GYPSY MUSIC STREET

a daughter journeys to her mother's

shattered world, a true story of love and

irrevocable loss

Roberta Dietzen

For Sylvia,
Roberta Dietzen

Gypsy Music Street

All Rights Reserved

Copyright © 2012 by Roberta Dietzen.

For information address the author at rldietzen@comcast.net

ISBN: 978-0-615-84314-8

Cover design by Serge Isaacson, Zanzinato Design.

DEDICATION

For Mother

CONTENTS

ACKNOWLEDGMENTS

Many thanks and much love to my awesome family, especially to my husband Mark who gave me the courage and confidence to write this story. Stoically, he also provided the computer skills to help me finish the project.

For my children, I am forever grateful; their steadfast love and encouragement is a gift. Matthew's insightful editing advice was invaluable. Jolie, with much patience, spent hours restoring many of the old photographs. Hedy's remarkable illustrations, a work in progress, will soon be a meaningful addition to Gypsy Music Street.

1 The Vine

The look on my mother's face said she went somewhere. Where will always remain a mystery, but I like to think that she finally went home. And in my grief, I was compelled to find her. I gathered together Mother's dreams and made them my own. I returned to Munkacs.

And just before I left her town, I cut a grapevine that was growing near the new little synagogue, carefully wrapped it in a moist paper towel, and placed it in a plastic bottle. In the beginning, it sprouted a few new buds and I was so hopeful it would give off fresh shoots and flourish in my garden back home. A lush green pergola of grapes like all the other pergolas we saw as we sped through the Carpathian countryside. Every year we would harvest the rich, red grapes and make wine. I dreamed that my family and I would sit outside on warm summer evenings, speak about Mother and drink the sweet fragrant wine.

But just as the thick colorful threads of Jewish culture were destroyed, the vine slowly withered and died.

2 Destiny

The last two years of her life Mother languished in a nursing home; one of the few residents, who alone, could get on the elevator in her wheelchair and make their way down to the lobby. There, she and I would sit together at least twice a week and pass the time, struggling to make conversation when there was so little to say.

She wore her permanent look of misery and I wore mine of impatience and boredom. That Mother had a sharp and clear mind was a mixed blessing, for although we could still speak to one another, she spoke primarily of her death. Her fear pervasive, she felt its tentacles pulling as everyday her energy diminished. "I don't live and I don't die."

One day she had an epiphany, "I've come to the conclusion that people with Alzheimer's are lucky," she declared in her heavy Hungarian accent, "They don't know vat's going on." The "W" sound was impossible for Mother to pronounce. At this point in her life, being in a fog about her future was what she considered luck.

And she was still so funny, wondering out loud, asking the rhetorical question, "Vat's my destiny," as she wryly observed those around her. "Most of the people here are already on the other side," she often remarked. During the activity sessions, the bored activity director would yawn and toss a ball to "someone on the other side" and watch it slowly roll away from a wet, vacant stare.

Mother tried to make herself presentable. She still had her thin hair dyed strawberry blonde, she refused to go gray, and wore it up in a French roll as she had for years. Dainty earrings, coral lipstick and compact powder, which I replaced every month from the drugstore, completed her look. It seemed no one hated being old as much as Mother. "I scare myself ven I look in the mirror, vat happens to a person!"

And so we passed the afternoons of my visits. Drinking coffee together, her large frame seated slumped shouldered in her chair, Mother complained. I listened helplessly. Because she still had her wits, she could advocate for herself and make demands. "I think you'd like to kill me," she told one particularly hateful nurse."

"You're smart," the nurse replied.

Of course the food was horrid. "All they give you is pork." Time crawled as I stole peaks at my watch and the obligatory hour slowly passed. I tried to redirect her complaints, I spoke about the family. My children, or even better her sister Greta's family; somehow, their lives were always more interesting and enviable than those of her own.

After we exhausted our discussion of all the various family members our conversation would turn to Mother's past, and these were the conversations I enjoyed the most. She spoke of Munkacs, "the little Paris of the East," a town located in what was then Czechoslovakia. Munkacs is the Hungarian name, but there are numerous ways to spell this town, several variations of "Mukacevo" depending on whether one is Ukrainian, Russian or Czech. Mother described Munkacs as a small modern city nestled in the foothills of the Carpathian Mountains, the town where she was born and raised. "A charming city," she told me. One could see the mountains in the distance and she would walk there picking wildflowers, mushrooms and medicinal herbs. The Latorica River where the townspeople swam and bathed and washed their clothes slowly flowed through the center of town. There was a movie theater and a progressive secondary school called the Hebrew Gymnasium. Munkacs had a large population of Hasidic, Orthodox and Zionist Jews who endlessly squabbled among themselves, but coexisted peacefully with the gentiles and gypsies in this part of the world.

On Shabbos, the Jewish stores closed and the people hurried home from work before sundown to enjoy a traditional Sabbath meal. Her father Markus often brought guests to dinner, sometimes a traveling salesman. "No one should be alone on Shabbos," he said. But when Shabbos ended, young boys and girls would gather and stroll the Korzo, the main street, flirting, talking, laughing; enjoying their carefree and fleeting youth.

Mother reminisced about her large religious family. She was one of nine children, with two older brothers, five younger brothers, and one older sister. The Lehrer family lived among many musicians on Zenez Ut, Music Street. The locals called this road Gypsy Music Street.

She remembered World War I and the soldiers with their guns running through the streets. Her mother sent the children to hide in the attic. Her father Markus put flour in his beard to make himself look like an old man, so he would not be conscripted in the army.   In 1926, at sixteen years old, Mother began working at the drugstore in town. She always walked home for lunch. It was just a short distance on the old cobbled streets where waiting for her was the main meal of the day that her mother had prepared.

* * *

At twenty-six years old, Mother left Europe in 1937 with fond memories. As part of the Austro-Hungarian Empire and then Czechoslovakia, the Jews of Munkacs enjoyed the same civil liberties as the gentiles. It was a progressive city where people respected each other. There was plenty of poverty, but pogroms happened in other places. They were unheard of in Munkacs.

Mother left behind her parents and her younger brothers, not realizing at the time she would never see most of her family again. Her ninety year old grandmother, who was living far away, rode all night on a train so she could be there to say good-bye. My mother's father took her to the train station and there he told his wife, "Take a good look at her because you're never going to see her again. "

"How did he know," Mother wondered out loud over the years.

Markus stepped up and onto the train to accompany his daughter for just a few stops before he finally had to say good-bye and get off. This part of the story, which I had heard so many times, touched me to my core. That her father, rode with Mother on the train just so he could be with her a little longer, to look at her and hear her voice once more before she took her long journey, always broke my heart.

It was a cloudy, gray afternoon just a few months before Mother died at ninety-six, so frail but still fighting with her inner, iron strength to live, live, live. Sitting in her wheelchair, she looked at me as she lifted her hand to her heart. "My parents, what happened to them, it hurts, it's always with me." How those words cut.

My mother departed from Europe a year before the war broke out, she never experienced the horrors of the concentration camps. She left for a better life. Irving and Greta, two of her older siblings had immigrated to the United States earlier, and they were waiting in Chicago for her arrival. She had worked hard and saved her money and dreamed about a future filled with opportunity. But in doing so, she left her parents, several brothers and scores of relatives behind. "Hitler's coming," a neighbor pointedly remarked to her father one day across the fence. She never foresaw the devastation her family would endure, yet she believed she had abandoned them to die alone.

Markus Lehrer

3 Grandmother

An old framed black and white photograph of my grandmother, Roza Salomon Lehrer, sits on a table in my living room. When I walk by this photo during the day I don't look directly at it, although I am constantly aware of its presence. Sometimes though, I do stop and pick up the picture and look closely. I see a sturdy woman wearing a simple work dress. A ruffled white apron is tied at the waist, a hand on a hip. A white kerchief covers what I know was shorn carrot colored hair. These are her work clothes. There is a small black cat hiding behind one foot and in the background, an old weathered wooden door. Flowers and vines grow on the side of a fence. Morning glories perhaps. "It's too bad," I think to myself because I can't quite make out her face. Blue eyes are scrunched up a bit, her features somewhat distorted in the direct sunlight. It is a photograph of a woman who might have lived to be an old lady like so many other women in our family.

"My mother was a slave," mom often remarked as I was growing up.

Sometimes she hired peasant girls to help with the

mountain of laundry, but most of the time she struggled on her own with the tremendous workload of having a large family. There were seven boys and two girls and no modern conveniences; no dishwasher or washing machine. Soap was made from ashes, floors were scrubbed on one's hands and knees, clean rags were used as menstrual pads.

"She would lay down to rest a little on Shabbos," Mother said.

This was a woman who should have been allowed to cook and clean and wash, to continue to nurture her family; to be a grandmother I would have known and loved and would have returned that love. She longed to see her grandchildren, those that had already been born far away in the States.

Whenever she saw the neighbors with their grandchildren, she jealously cried, "Why can't I see my grandchildren?!"

And so I told my mother as she sat in her wheelchair on that cold cloudy day, "Yes, I feel it too;" an ever present pain, sharp and vivid, sometimes dull and gauzy, but always a feeling I carry, and cannot shake.

4 The Little Paris of the East

The idyllic picture my mother painted took shape in my head. My whole life I heard the stories. The beautiful mountains, the river that flowed through the town, the close-knit Jewish community. "So if it was so wonderful, why did you leave?" I once asked her.

"For a better life," my mother always said.

Because even though Munkacs was a small charming town, the opportunities were limited. Everyone dreamed of coming to the United States where the streets were paved with gold. The United States was a large, pulsating, dynamic world where endless opportunities existed, even for a young European woman with no education.

The Lehrers were a middle-class family typical of the Orthodox Jews in that area. Everyone was an observant Jew in Munkacs, or at least gave the appearance of being such. Married women cut and covered their hair. It never really made much sense to Mother.

"They cut off their nice hair and then put on a wig to look attractive," she didn't understand.

A large family of nine children, also typical of that time, birth control was not an option for Orthodox women and my grandmother would cry when she discovered herself to be pregnant yet again.

"She sent all of us outside in the yard when the new baby was coming, we could hear the screams from the house," Mother remembered.

It was a hard life to raise such a big family in that time and place. Rezsi and Gitel were expected to help in the home. Grandmother would sometimes remark, "The two girls are worth more than all the boys! "

* * *

Markus, my grandfather was a businessman, a timber merchant. My mother described him as an honest man who sold wood to the movie theater in the city, the monastery on the hill at the edge of town and other small businesses in the area. And sometimes when he had difficulty collecting his money, he would send his oldest daughter Gitel the coquette, wearing her prettiest dress, to flirt with and finesse payment from these customers.

The Jews and the gentiles got along well together. There were not any overt signs of antisemitism while my mother was growing up. Occasionally a priest from the monastery visited her home where Grandma would serve him hot tea and they would sit together chatting. Only once, did Mother remember that neighbors backhanded remark: "Hitler's coming."

"My mother slaved day and night," Mom repeated many times throughout the years. It was arduous and endless work everyday raising such a large family and without modern conveniences or indoor plumbing. During the day, the family used the outhouse set back in the corner of the yard. "My father cursed," as he trudged through piles of snow on a frigid winter day. At night, chamber pots were brought out from under the beds to be used as needed. Sometimes my grandmother brought in a peasant girl from a nearby village to help with the laundry, but most of the time she worked alone, washing enormous stacks of clothes in tubs in the yard.

The average person owned but a few changes of clothes,

perhaps two or three outfits, but they were all custom-made by a tailor in town and all of excellent quality. The women went to a dressmaker where they chose a pattern and material of their liking. In all the old photographs, my mother looks so well dressed, of course wearing her best outfit for the photographer; her lovely dress trimmed with a lace collar and cuffs, beautifully accessorized with an antique beaded necklace.

"And what about bathing Mother," I would ask, "How did you bathe?"

"Who bathed," she would reply. No one bathed, at least as to what we consider bathing to be nowadays with indoor plumbing. "People sponged themselves, they took sponge baths." And during the hot summer months they "jumped in the river" where they would swim and cleanse themselves in the gentle, lazy Latorica. Sometimes, my mother would accompany Grandma to the mikvah, the ritual bath where observant Jewish women went to cleanse and purify themselves every month.

Renee seated on left; two friends; Greta standing on right.

5 Love

Invariably, our conversation would turn to Mother's love life. I wondered aloud why she had not married and settled down with a suitable husband to raise a family in Munkacs. Why had she not married younger as was customary for Eastern European Jewish women?

The lingering sorrow of her old romance with Blum Gyula resurfaced; an unrequited love. Mother set the scene for this story as she always did, by first recounting her almost complete lack of education, her "tragedy" as she called it. Her mother removed her from school after the second grade under the pretext of political changes affecting the school system.

"I never forgave her," she said forlornly sitting in her wheelchair just one month before she died.

She had been an excellent, smart student. She enjoyed school, especially learning Russian. Good with languages, she began to teach one of her younger brothers to speak Russian as well.

But she was needed at home to help with all the chores. Rising early in the morning she scoured floors, and in the evening she washed heaping loads of dishes. When she was working at the drugstore she walked home for lunch, and in that short hour she was still expected to help; shining eleven pairs of shoes all lined up in a row waiting to be cleaned.

But even though Mother had no formal schooling, it seemed she was only attracted to men who did; men who had an advanced and formal education, men who were engineers.

This was her misfortune, for Mother was a smart person who never had the opportunity to realize her potential.

"I felt it my whole life," she said.

She was drawn to a type of man to whom, in her eyes, she had nothing to offer. She was not worthy of them. When she spoke of love, it was always about Blum Gyula. An odd name I thought. It was only much later I discovered Hungarians always use the surname first. His name, translated in English, is Julius Blum and so not such a strange name at all.

Blum Gyula was an engineer from a "good" family. He was

tall, handsome, had a thick head of hair. He worked in Budapest or Prague and saw Mother only on the occasions when he came to town to visit his family. I don't know how serious he was about her. I know they would promenade up and down the Korzo. Sometimes they hiked into the foothills of the nearby Carpathians and picked wildflowers. I would later discover that these mountains were as lush, green and beautiful as mother had described.

But for whatever reason, this romance never progressed to a marriage proposal. And it was for the best. If Blum Gyula had been in love with my mother enough to marry her, she would have remained with him in Europe and most probably perished.

6 Marriage

It's the summer of 1942, and in an old black and white photograph there is Mother sitting in a rowboat on a lake in the Catskill Mountains. She is wearing a matching two-piece floral short set; her long hair pinned up on the sides, flows down her back. Next to her is a handsome dark haired man. They are embracing; gazing into each others' eyes, smiling. Six months later they will be married.

In 1937, Mother arrived in Chicago and Rezsi became Renee. Gitel had already changed her name to Greta. Their Americanized names sounded far less foreign and somewhat more glamorous than their real names. Mother always said she never liked the name Renee. Greta had chosen it for her, so she

took it.

After a few years of living in a small room behind Greta's laundry, Mother was unhappy. Even though she was surrounded by family members, she did not hesitate to move to New York when an uncle told her of his connections in Manhattan.

"I put a newspaper under my arm and vent out looking for verk," she remembered.

And she did find work in a variety of factories. She loved the excitement of the city where she found an apartment with two other young Hungarian girls. Together the roommates went to dances looking for romance, but by this time, the war was well under way and there were few desirable men at these affairs. The young and healthy were off fighting, only the elderly, unappealing "fellas" would ask for an occasional dance. The girls became disheartened.

During the summers, Mother worked as a waitress at a resort in the Catskill Mountains. One early evening, as she walked to town to see a movie by herself, the man who would become my father pulled up alongside in his car and invited himself to join her. George Stern was vacationing with his mother at the same resort; an artist who spent his days painting the local scenery, he had taken notice of Renee.

Gyorgy was handsome, Jewish, and a talented Hungarian artist from Szekesfehervar, a town near Budapest. They both spoke the same language. The other young women at the hotel were jealous of the attention George gave Renee.

So it was okay that he wasn't the love of her life, she was anxious to settle down and start a family. She wasn't getting any younger, it was "slim pickings"; she accepted my father's proposal and they married within a few months.

7 Growing Up

As a young girl growing up in Chicago, I always sensed how different my mother was from other mothers. She was several years older than them, and older when I was born. My first memory of her was of a matronly woman, she was no longer young. She didn't wear Capri pants in the summer or know how to play cards. She was from the old country with old world ways and when I excitedly told her about the onset of my period, she quickly reached out and slapped me in the face. I was shocked, distressed.

"Why did you do that?!" I cried.

"It's the tradition, you're a woman now. You must be careful."

When a new friend would phone our home for the first time and hear Mother's heavy Hungarian accent, they would always ask, "Was that your grandmother"?

It seemed Mother was forever in the kitchen cooking. Jumbled ingredients and utensils covered the counters; the stove cluttered with several steaming pots and pans. The clean-up was always so much harder than it had to be, for as she cooked, my mother would transfer the food from one size pot to another. Her first choice of cookware was always too small or too big for whatever she was making.

And it was always the wonderful aroma of hearty, homemade Jewish soups and Hungarian stews that greeted me whenever I arrived home from school. Truly a talented cook, everything my mother prepared was delicious. "You have to have a feel for it," she would say. I didn't appreciate the effort, the love that went into making those meals. I turned up my nose at the stuffed cabbage. These were things I took for granted. I thought every mother cooked this way. It was only when I grew up and peered into other kitchens and saw them sterile and lacking in so many ways that I discovered my mother's way of nourishing and nurturing her family was more the exception than the rule. Her meals were to be treasured.

* * *

Even as a young child, I sensed a dark cloud hovering over Mother. Year by year, I slowly learned the history surrounding the fate of her family. I have a memory.

At seven or eight years old, the elementary school chose me and a handful of other students to participate in a German language program. I remember feeling very special because of this. At the time, this was a unique program since second languages were rarely offered in the Chicago public school system at the elementary level. After I learned a few basic phrases, I came home and proudly started speaking to my mother in German. "Wie geht es ihnen?" "How are you?" I asked.

Her response was a shock. Instead of some interest or delight in my new ability, she became agitated. She started to talk about how the Germans had killed her parents.

"They told them they were going to take a shower and then they gassed them." She covered her crying face and ran into the bedroom as I stood alone and confused in the living room.

I never spoke German in the house again. Deflated, my desire to learn the language disappeared. Mother couldn't tolerate the sound of German. When she overheard a woman speaking it to her child in the grocery store she cried out uncontrollably. "Why are you teaching her that horrible language?"

8 Michael

At forty-three years old Mother found herself pregnant, and it was a pregnancy that was neither wanted nor planned.

"I was happy with the two girls," she always said.

Yet, when she phoned my father from the hospital to say they now had a son, she was overjoyed.

"It's a boy, it's a boy," Dad shouted out thrilled, as he jumped up and down in our tiny one bedroom apartment in Great Neck, Long Island.

But the initial excitement quickly turned to sorrow. Michael had my father's features, his dark brown hair and hazel eyes, only those features were distorted. The pediatrician, Dr. Petrover, explained Down's syndrome to my parents. Michael had an extra chromosome. He would be retarded. Some doctors called him a Mongoloid; this term was acceptable in those days.

Michael had a heart defect, not uncommon in those children; he was not expected to live past the age of five. The doctors encouraged my parents to institutionalize Michael immediately, before they became too attached. But my parents could not bring themselves to do it.

"When Michael was born, I died," Mother said, and she began to go to the movies alone, sit in the darkness and escape into the story unfolding on the screen. As a young child, Michael appeared happy and playful, but he had no playmates. Our neighbors made sure their children avoided him as if he was contaminated with a horrible contagious disease.

The grammar school sat across the street from our house. Mother looked out through the window and watched little boys walking to school in the morning and playing at recess.

"Those boys are Michael's age," she said.

Then, as now, there were limited resources and few options available for children like Michael, especially for families with a lower income. In the beginning he attended day programs that provided him some schooling, but after awhile, he would always refuse to go. Each morning it was a struggle to force him to get up, dressed, and on time for the special bus; he preferred to stay home and watch television.

At sixteen, the hole in Michael's heart was repaired and he continued to live at home. But as he grew older and larger, he became increasingly difficult to handle, the disparity between his size and low I.Q. more evident. His little boy happy-go-lucky behavior turned into stubbornness and temper tantrums. My aging parents finally realized they needed to get help. But good facilities for the mentally impaired were in short supply; it was only the wealthier families who could afford to place their children in a suitable residence. And so, for lack of money, my parents struggled for years with the politics of the system.

At one point, it seemed that Michael was content, settled in a private residential facility located in a quiet suburb of Chicago. But after a year, when he turned twenty-one, he was made to leave. Those were the rules. It didn't matter that his I.Q was that of a young child.

The endless searching for a suitable facility among the limited choices continued for years. Either Michael didn't meet the requirements, my family couldn't afford it, or the residence itself was so awful, it couldn't possibly meet with my parent's approval.

Eventually Michael was placed in a small group home, part

of the Kiley Developmental Center in a suburb more than 30 miles from my parent's apartment. It wasn't ideal and it wasn't home, but my parents were satisfied because Michael appeared to be relatively content. They became involved with the parents' association, annually selling boxes of nuts and organizing mostaccolli dinners to raise funds. And always there was the uncertainty about whether or not the State would close the facility. There was never enough money and the governor of Illinois would threaten and the anxious parents would meet, discuss and try to figure out what to do. Stick together, write letters, on and on for years and years. But through all this interminable aggravation, Mother especially, prevailed.

My father died in 1976, and it became more difficult for Mother to make her weekly visits to Michael. As she had never learned to drive, she now became dependent on other people to provide her with a ride. Mark and I helped her as much as we could; sometimes she persuaded another relative or a neighbor to make the trip. But through the years, when no one was available to drive her, she alone would take a bus, transfer on to the train and from the train take a taxi to the Kiley Center; burdened with a cane in one hand and carrying satchels of food and clothes in the other, she managed. And every two months, like clock work, Mother would bring Michael home for the weekend. Nothing stopped her or stood in her way.

"You'd better have your baby this weekend," she told me as my due date approached for my third child.

She wanted to care for my two older children while I was in the hospital, but she had other pressing matters; it was almost time to bring Michael home for his visit. So I did what I was told. I went into a natural labor and then gave birth to my beautiful daughter Jolie.

And then at the end of the week, Mother went to the Kiley Center to fetch Michael. It was always easy to bring him home; eager, he was waiting and dressed.

"He needs a break," Mother always said.

Michael enjoyed relaxing, watching T.V. and eating home cooked meals. Mother would try and coax him out for a walk or a burger but usually he was reluctant to leave the apartment. At the end of the weekend, when it was time for Michael to return to the institution, there was the same big problem. He became agitated

as the time of his departure drew near, would rage and bellow and

refuse to get dressed. This is when the "troops" were called in.

Pleading phone calls were made to Mark. Mother couldn't handle

Michael, she needed muscle. Mark would always drive into the

city from the suburbs, go up to the apartment, stand at the foot of

Michael's bed and just talk to him. Six feet and four inches and an

authoritative demeanor convinced him. Michael calmly got

dressed and Mark drove him back to Kiley.

"That's the last time, I'm never going to bring him home

again," Mother always said with such resolve.

But after the next two months were gone, she had

forgotten her resolve and the cycle was repeated. This continued

until she was 89 years old. By then she no longer had the

strength for his home visits anymore, yet she still continued to see

him weekly if her health permitted. Afraid when she died that there

would be no one to look after Michael, I reassured her that I would

do my best as his guardian, but still she worried.

It was a cold, frosty morning in January, 2000. Sitting at my

kitchen table with my sister, we were drinking coffee. Junie, following her divorce, had just moved back to Chicago from New York. She was living with us until she found herself a job and an apartment. The phone rang, I could barely hear a woman's voice; someone with an Indian accent was calling from the Kiley Center.

"Something terrible happened," the woman said.

"Excuse me, what did you say? I can't hear you," I replied.

"Something terrible happened," she repeated more loudly. "Michael died this morning. An aide found him collapsed on the floor."

"Please don't call my mother," I begged. "I want to tell her myself."

In shock, Junie and I drove to the city. Michael was dead at 46 years old. He had lived much longer than his pediatricians had predicted. He hadn't looked well the last time I saw him a few weeks before he died, there were vague complaints of stomach pains and his skin was sallow. He never could articulate what he was feeling.

* * *

Mother buzzed us into her apartment surprised at our unannounced weekday visit. She opened the door with a big grin and hurriedly turned back to the television. We had interrupted her time with Maury Povich. Engrossed in a salacious segment, she muttered something about the story she was watching: "They don't know who the father of the pregnant woman is."

As Mother sat back down in her worn blue slip-covered recliner, Junie shut off the T.V. She knelt down, took Mother's hands in her own, and we told her.

"Michael! My Michael?" She cried out in disbelief." What happened to him?"

The next hour remains a blur as we tried to comfort her. Calls were made to the Kiley Center, questions were asked. We wanted more information. I called a funeral home and began to make the necessary arrangements; the burial process had begun. Because Michael had died so suddenly, the county coroner requested an autopsy. Michael had an enlarged heart; the cause of death was heart disease.

Mother lived several years after Michael died. The

obsessive worry about him was replaced by an emptiness, a loneliness. "I think about Michael every day," she often said. Her focus, the center of her world had disappeared, and now the main reason to battle on in life was gone.

9 Seven Brothers

When the war broke out, Mother, Greta, and their eldest brother Irving were living safely in the United States. "We used to talk about bringing my parents out from Europe," Mother would sometimes quietly say to herself more than to anyone who might be listening. Another older brother Chaim, a Zionist, had immigrated to Israel a few years prior.

So what exactly did happen to the remainder of my mother's family? What happened to those handsome red-headed brothers, who from the old photographs, all bore a strong resemblance to one another? In the photos, they appear tall, fair-skinned, with small eyes, high cheekbones, and a long sharp nose. Their hair is thinning. "Unfortunately they lost most of their hair when they were still young," Mother would remember aloud.

A few conflicting stories had filtered down through the years. We know that several of the boys were taken, perhaps as early as 1941, into the Hungarian Labor Battalion. Two of the boys died in these forced slave labor camps, Joseph and Moshe Leibe. Mother thought she recognized one of her brothers laying dead in a photo. It was just one of the thousands of ghastly images released to the public. She never was sure it was him. Maybe it was Moishe Leibe, her favorite brother, the brother whom she felt close to. I never thought to ask which brother it might have been. Over the years she repeated, "Once I saw a picture, it looked like my brother, lying on the ground, dead."

The Lehrer Family, Mother on the left

And what of the others? Lipot, Harry and Yidel, these three did survive the war. Lipot escaped from the labor camp, hid out in the forest and fought with the partisans, of whom it was said they liked fighting alongside Jews as much as Jews liked pork. It was rumored that Lipot killed a man, perhaps a Nazi soldier, somewhere along the way. He came to Chicago, became successful in the nursing home business and never spoke about the past. He refused to speak Hungarian with his family.

Harry came to Chicago and lived with Greta, an arrangement which did not last long as it soon became evident that Harry was a broken man. Sullen, he refused to work. Sometimes he erupted in fits of rage. Once he emerged from the basement, his face blackened with coal. My Aunt Greta and Uncle Lipot were both struggling in their new country. They were each raising their own small children and trying to survive. They did not have the time or energy to cope with a sick brother. Harry was committed to Manteno, the Illinois State Mental Hospital, and he remained there for many years. Eventually, when the facility closed he was transferred to a nursing home in the Chicago area where he was institutionalized for the remainder of his life, forty years.

Once a doctor called from Manteno and informed the family that Harry should be released. "There's nothing wrong with him, he can go home now," the doctor said.

No one went for him. No one took him home. My mother made excuses, for she had a difficult time coping with the needs of my retarded brother.

"I didn't put him away, I've got Michael to care for. If he had parents to help, he wouldn't be there," she would always add.

Harry had suffered a nervous breakdown and the question was, if he had recovered enough to be released, why couldn't he just leave on his own? Pack his bags and walk away? He had nowhere to go and no means to support himself. He was a broken man and it was easier to stay in an institution where all his needs were met than to venture out into the world alone, without the support of his family.

Then there was Yidel. After the war, he remained in Europe and lived in Prague. He became involved in selling on the black market and as a result was imprisoned. By this time,

Czechoslovakia was firmly under the Soviet umbrella and ruled with the Communist iron fist. Terror and suspicion were rampant and illegal black market activities were not tolerated. Sometime, in the late 1950's or early 1960's, Uncle Lipot was finally able to save the money to go to Prague and bribe the Czech officials to release Yidel from prison. But it was too late. Yidel had lost his mind.

There were many stories surrounding his captivity. Yidel's captors beat him about the head. To torture him, they attached electrodes to his body and plunged him into water. So when Yidel finally moved to Chicago, he too was shattered, completely altered from the normal, happy brother my mother insisted she had left behind.

He moved into the basement of Greta's house, a tiny unfinished space near the laundry room, and lived there for forty years. He never learned English. He made no sense when he did speak Hungarian. No one saw him bathe. He refused to use soap. The Nazis had made soap from his parents, he said. He smelled bad. He drank too much whiskey he found at the nearby shul. But somehow, he was able to hold down a job and he worked as a night janitor in Chicago at Marshall Field's department store. He would take the elevated train late at night when all kinds of unsavory characters joined him on the platform. He was unafraid. "How can I be afraid after all that I went through during the war?" Yidel would say.

Only he alone knew exactly what those experiences were. So when Yidel got mugged and beaten, and it happened more than once, he continued to work the night shift regardless of the danger.

Yidel persevered, worked relentlessly and saved almost all his money. His teeth were broken and decayed and his suit and shoes tattered, but he still refused to spend any money on himself. He put some of the money in the bank and hoarded the rest, rumored to be in Aunt Greta's basement. Hidden and tucked away somewhere in the walls, "Yidel's money" was a frequent topic of speculation and gossip in the family.

Years later, when he finally died in a nursing home, it was said that his money was long gone, spent on his care. And it was not for anyone to dispute, for it was not in Mother's basement in which he had lived all those long, lonely years.

Yidel on the Korzo

* * *

What became of my grandparents? Again, there were

conflicting stories. My grandfather Markus was originally from

Galicia. When the Hungarian fascists occupied Munkacs in 1939,

within a short time, all the Galicianers who had not obtained

Hungarian citizenship and did not have proper documentation

were deported to the East. However, it was reported by

eyewitnesses who had escaped from these deportations that the

Jews had been taken off the trains at a certain point and gunned down by the SS who were waiting for the transport.

It is believed that my grandfather Markus was taken at this time, forced onto a wagon and driven to the rail station. He said good-bye to his wife and apologized for his bad temper, for she would often stand between him and her boys, trying to shield them when he took off his belt in a rage. My mother only told me this story once. She thought the Nazis shot her father. Someone from the family, perhaps her brother Lipot, had seen his father taken away and had recounted what happened. My mother didn't dwell on this story, and at the time of its telling I could see how painful it was for her to talk about it. I remember questioning her further but she did not want to continue the conversation and I let it go.

My cousin told me a different version. My grandmother and grandfather were taken away at the same time. They walked away together holding hands. In the spring of 1944, the Munkacs Jews were rounded up and driven from their homes and into a few streets designated as their ghetto near the Latorica River. They lived in this ghetto for a short time before they were marched to the brickyard and locked into a warehouse without enough food, water or proper sanitation. This brickyard was situated on the rail line and it was the place where the Jews were forced onto the cattle cars bound for Auschwitz.

At the end of the war, when the Germans and Hungarian fascists had fled Trans-Carpathia,   the surviving Lehrer brothers returned to Munkacs. They, like many other Jewish survivors returned to their homes with great hopes of finding other loved family members and friends. Yidel, Harry and Lipot returned to their home on Music Street and found everyone gone. Only the matzas and the Passover food, cold soup and spoiled meat were still there on the stove, for it was Passover when the Jews were forced into the ghetto.

My grandmother was still cooking, baking and trying to observe Pesach even while the dark threatening clouds were closing in on her and her family. Mother often reminisced about the family Seders. Her mother would don her best dress and wear a wig in place of her daily kerchief. Her father would proudly put on his kitel, the white cotton robe worn in honor of the religious holidays. He would take his place at the head of the table surrounded by his family, recline on a large pillow as was the tradition, and recount the Passover story until midnight. When my grandfather opened the door to let in Elijah's ghost to drink from the glass of wine waiting for him on the table, his children would shudder in fear.

My grandmother had to leave her home so quickly, with only fifteen minutes warning, the home where she had raised her family for so many years; there was no time to take much. Only to leave the house she had spent years cleaning, in complete chaos and disarray. And the food, the symbolic Jewish food, remained behind.

10 The Baby

Not long before Mother died, I believe I found the answer to what became of her brother Joseph's baby son, only two or three years old in 1944 when the Hungarian Jews were murdered. I don't know his name. I only know he had curly reddish blonde hair, blue eyes and fair skin like many other members of Mother's family. Over the years, Mother often spoke about Joseph. His family called him by his Jewish name, Yossel. I didn't know much about Yossel, just that he was a dental technician who made teeth. "He was the smartest of the seven brothers," Mother recalled. He married a teacher.

In 1941 the Munkatabor, the Hungarian Labor Battalion, forced the young Jewish men to leave their families and work as slaves. Beaten, humiliated, starved, abused in every imaginable way, most did not survive.

"They were worked to death," Mother said.

Joseph's wife, whose name I did not learn until a few years ago, gave the baby boy to my grandmother Roza. My grandmother needed to take care of the little boy while his mother "went to work."

Mother brooded over the years, "What happened to the baby?" Blonde and blue eyed, he did not look particularly Jewish. Maybe a kind gentile neighbor took him and protected him and he survived the war. Perhaps he still lives today, knowing or not knowing his true identity.

A year before Mother died, she startled me with a new fact about this story. We were passing time in the nursing home's lobby drinking coffee and chatting. I was sitting on the couch, she was sitting in her wheelchair. It was a dim wintry Chicago afternoon and the cold gray seeped through the large glass windows. Nice windows, but not much of a view I thought; parked cars in the lot and a frequent flow of emergency ambulances bringing people in and taking them away on stretchers. The place where Mother sat and reminisced. Once again, her thoughts turned to the baby boy and what happened to him.

"Tell me more about the boy's mother," I asked.

"Blanca," Mother said. Yes, I saw her once in New York after the war."

I was stunned. After all the years of hearing this story, I never thought to ask about the fate of the boy's mother. I always assumed she perished in the Holocaust. But she had survived. Mother had seen her alive after the war, a staggering revelation. She remembered almost nothing about the details of their meeting and they did not meet one another again.

* * *

Soon another piece of this puzzle would be discovered. A first cousin Barbara, who at the time lived in Montreal and to whom I had not spoken in many years, contacted me and my other Chicago cousins. Barbara was the only daughter of Uncle Lipot, one of the seven brothers. From all the cousins, she was the one who had been raised strictly Orthodox. After her marriage, she eventually moved to Canada and no one heard much from her over the years. Barbara successfully raised four children, but after her parents died, followed by her young husband who passed away from a tragic illness, Barbara needed to reconnect with family. She came for a visit and we spent a wonderful few days reflecting about our youth and growing up in Chicago.

During one of our conversations, Barbara mentioned

Blanca had once contacted her. Years ago, living in New York City as a young wife and mother with a small child, she had received an unexpected phone call from Blanca. Over the phone, Blanca explained she had been married to her Uncle Joseph before the war and she wanted to meet with her niece. How she found her phone number or why exactly she wanted to meet will always be a mystery.

Barbara strapped three year old Ariela into a baby carrier and took the subway to meet Blanca in Harlem. I never learned much about this meeting. Barbara's memory was vague. She remembered only that Blanca worked as a puppeteer. She mentioned that she had had a child about the same age as Ariela before the war.

When Barbara's parents, my Aunt Esther and Uncle Lipot, both survivors themselves, learned about the meeting they were not happy. They never told their daughter the reason, but they discouraged her from having any further contact with Blanca.

I then began to ask myself, how did Blanca survive the war and her child most certainly die? Where was she working when only the men were forced into the Hungarian slave labor battalions?

I started to read more about the deportations of the Jewish people. I studied *The Auschwitz Album*, a book of photographs that documents the arrival of a transport of Hungarian Jews from Bilke, a town not far from Munkacs. Taken with a hidden camera, these poignant photos reveal groups of mothers and young children. But one also sees very old women with young children. These must be the grandmothers and their grandchildren. So where are the mothers? Why are they missing from many of these pictures? These old women look too frail to walk. How do they have the energy to care for these young children? But in the pictures, one sees an effort has been made. Their coats are buttoned against the spring cold of 1944. Scarves are carefully tied over the heads and under the chins, tucked behind the necks and into the backs of the little girls' coats. Boys clutch their granny's' hands. Where are the mothers?

I learned what happened when the cattle cars arrived in Auschwitz. After three excruciatingly long days of terrible deprivation; no food, no water, no fresh air, no room to rest or relieve oneself, helpless but to stand so close and suffer together in the dark and see the old and sick die because many could not tolerate these inhumane conditions, the doors finally opened and the dazed people began to exit. And where did I read that most of the women from Munkacs went mad on the train?

It was then that the Sonderkommandos, the Jews forced to do the Nazis' gruesome work of deceiving the new arrivals and then disposing of the bodies, quickly entered the train and moved among the young mothers who were holding babies or the hands of their young ones. They whispered urgently, "Give your children to your mother and let your mother watch the children while you work. You will see your babies later." Some of these prisoners were more brutally honest. "Give your child to your mother and save yourself."

It happened over and over again. The mothers, confused and exhausted did what they were told. They did what they believed was best and they separated themselves from their children. The babies went with their grandmothers, to the right, to die. The mothers went to the left, to work and struggle and maybe survive the hell that lay ahead.

Now I imagined "What happened to the baby." Blanca

and her son were traveling in the cattle car with my grandmother. The families always tried to stay together if possible, the only source of comfort in the nightmare unfolding around them. Upon arriving, Blanca gave her beautiful curly blonde haired and blue eyed baby boy to Roza and "went to work." My grandmother and the baby perished and Blanca survived. Lipot and Esther must have known the truth and it was too painful. They did not want their daughter to have a relationship with Blanca because they could not bear to remember why she was alive, and grandma Roza and the baby were dead.

My grandmother was in her early sixties in 1944. She would have been gassed regardless of holding the baby. At sixty, the Nazis regarded the individual too old to work; worthless, useless. These elderly Jews were exterminated, burned alive in large open fiery pits when the crematoriums were not enough to accommodate the thousands of corpses. The living as well as the dead were thrown into these graves. Old, young, truckloads of babies, there are eyewitness accounts of this happening to the Hungarian Jews who were deported in May, 1944.

11 Aunt Esther

My lovely petite Aunt Esther was from Satu Mare, Romania, a town located just over the Hungarian border. I remember her dark brown eyes, tiny nose and short dark brown hair neatly styled, she was always so well-groomed. It was only from the expression on her face, the way she would look off into the distance and sigh sometimes, that I knew she had many sad secrets and memories.

She had met my Uncle Lipot in a displaced persons camp at the war's end and they had married quickly, for men and women who met in these DP camps often married without a long courtship. Once they realized their families had been decimated, and that they were very alone in the world, they were eager to seek solace and comfort from each other. Marriage meant having someone with whom to start life over, to once again have a family and bring children into the world. Children who would themselves procreate and bring more children into the world so that the Jewish people would continue to exist; to survive and flourish and prosper. These survivors drew their strength from the memory of their loved ones who had suffered so needlessly. These memories gave them energy to go on with life, to ensure their families did not die in vain. Their names and faces would be forever reflected in the future generations.

Aunt Esther and Uncle Lipot married and came to the United States. They had one child, a daughter, Barbara. Lipot became a wealthy businessman. My uncle raised his only daughter to be very religious, an Orthodox Jew. It seemed all that he had endured during the war did not destroy his faith and he wanted to ensure that Barbara embraced this faith, this way of life, as well.

Barbara knew almost nothing of what her father had suffered during the war, I learned. He never talked about the past and told people, if asked, he had immigrated to the U.S. before the war.

Because of Mother's stories, I knew more about Uncle Lipot's life than did his own daughter. He escaped the Hungarian slave labor battalion, he killed a man, and he fought and hid with the partisans in the forest. Through cunning and sheer luck, he survived the war. But it was his wife, my gentle soft spoken Aunt

Esther, who revealed one of her most chilling experiences more than twenty years after it had occurred.

Aunt Esther was hosting a bridal shower in her home. I can no longer remember for whom the shower was being held, it was that long ago. On a beautiful, sunny spring day, all the family and friends were gathered to open the gifts and celebrate. A few of us were together in the kitchen and Aunt Esther was there as well looking off into the distance. Her brows were knitted together, her thoughts elsewhere.

Suddenly she looked at me and exclaimed, "I was naked Bobbie, I was naked. I was the next in line but the gas chamber was full. It was stuffed with people."

This, from my aunt who always spoke so little and in short, hushed and incomplete sentences when she did. Shocked, I replied "oh!" and hoped it was said with an appropriate tone, for how could anyone understand how to respond to such a statement, so incongruous to the lovely day and happy occasion. I was twenty-one years old then, but I suddenly understood these memories were always and forever just below the surface for my aunt. She carried them around at all times, every moment of her waking consciousness and perhaps in her dreams. There was no respite from the horror, no reprieve. When she woke and ate breakfast. When she shopped and cooked and cleaned. When she worked with the residents in my uncle's nursing home. She could never forget. If she kept herself very busy, it was easier on some days to repress the memories. They were always there of course, but lurking a little farther in the distance. On other days, something would happen to trigger their sudden remembrance and there was no holding them back as they rushed in and flooded her mind. She had no choice but to embrace these memories, remember and grieve.

The Hungarian Jews were deported in the spring of 1944. This was spring again, more than twenty-five years later. Perhaps it was the same month, or the way the air smelled and the sun shone that lovely day that made her remember in a way that compelled her to share her thoughts. To speak out from her silence, and even then, when I understood so little, I was honored she had chosen me to listen.

12   A Neighbor from Turka

During the late 70's and early 80's, I lived in Highland Park, Illinois on the North Shore of Chicago where I still reside today. At that time, we had bought our first home on Pleasant Street. It was a modest house, a small English Tudor that had suffered neglect at the hands of various renters. I saw through the neglect, and with my husband and his father's help, our "fixer upper" was eventually transformed into a charming and cozy home we knew it could become.

I loved everything about our neighborhood; the mix of smaller, more modest homes where children played outside on the front lawn and neighbors would stop and chat with each other. The streets were shaded with mature trees and the location was ideal. The train that took Mark to his job in the city was just around the corner. The grocery store, the grammar school, the playground were all within easy walking distance.

As my husband began to travel for work more and more, my widowed mother frequently came up from the city on the train to spend time with the children and me. A mutually beneficial relationship, we alleviated our loneliness being together. The children became very attached to their grandmother as she helped me care for them. And what a tremendous help she was. As soon as she entered my home, it was as if a ton of bricks were lifted from my shoulders. She walked into the kitchen and immediately took charge; prepared dinner, bathed the kids, folded laundry, did whatever needed to be done and thoroughly enjoyed doing it. She felt useful and appreciated and oh yes, I did appreciate her help so much.

On warm sunny days, Mom and I often stood outside on the sidewalk to watch over the children while they played. It was there that we became acquainted with Jerry, an elderly and outgoing neighbor who lived just a few doors from me. Jerry worked around the house in the spring and summer, so it was natural we would sometimes stop and make small talk. As we chatted, I noticed Jerry had an accent and we soon discovered he was from Turka, a town in Ukraine not too far from Munkacs. Jerry and Mother were from the same part of the world, a distant remote place impossible to visit at this point. A place that for me, could only exist in my imagination, conjured from the frequent stories Mother told over and over again.

When we first met Jerry in 1979, he told us he had not returned to Turka since the war. Ukraine was part of the Soviet Union and this area was off limits for travel. He intimated that he had done some intelligence work for the Americans during the war and his presence would not be welcome in the Soviet Union. As he was a bit vague about his past, I sensed his reluctance to say too much and I did not press him. Jerry and Mother met, exchanged pleasantries, acknowledged that they were from the same area, and nothing more was said between them.

Jerry was a gentile and Mother was a Jew. Although they were both from the same part of the world, I assumed Jerry had not suffered the same persecution and loss of family as had my mother. It would be more than twenty years before I would learn the tragic truth of Jerry's life during those nightmare years of war.

13 Expatriates

Late spring of 1984, six weeks after the birth of my third child Jolie, Mark came home from work and announced an opportunity he had been offered; a job in Geneva, Switzerland, how could we refuse?! We had often dreamed about and discussed the possibility of living abroad as expatriates and now here was the chance. So maybe it was not the best time with a brand new baby and two other small children but we decided to take this opportunity anyway. We moved to Switzerland and remained there for five years. I tell people those years away were a true learning experience, for I did learn so much about other lands, languages and cultures in addition to discovering much about myself.

Living in a foreign country was much more challenging than I first believed it would be. Mark and I had traveled extensively for his job. In the late 70's and early 80's, we had moved to Alabama on two separate occasions for a few years, and then to Texas. I assumed this would be a similar experience. But I was no longer living in "the good ole U.S.A." nor was I a tourist who could return home after a few weeks and regale my friends with my adventures. I was stuck in Switzerland. Yes stuck, as incongruous as that may sound, because living abroad was harder than I had ever imagined.

I was alone in a strange country with a young demanding family of three small children and a husband who traveled across Europe, the Middle East and Africa more than half the time while my elderly mother was living alone in Chicago. My sister and her family had moved to Ithaca, New York and were far away. Feeling guilty about this situation, we organized a wonderful visit for Mom. She would come to Geneva in the summer and we would show her the sights; all the natural beauty of our surroundings, the majestic mountains and lakes, the old picturesque villages. I was sure she would love it all.

I was mistaken. My mother was not someone to whom you could show a good time. Between the natural expense of living in Switzerland and the dollar's decline, she complained endlessly. "It's too expensive here, why is it so expensive? In Munkacs, a dollar was worth a lot!"

"Mother, that was fifty years ago. This is Geneva, the

Beverly Hills of Europe!" I tried to explain the situation over and over again, but my explanations were ignored.

Mother had to make her own good time in her own way and it took me years to understand this about her. Cooking, gardening, even grocery shopping. The simple pleasures were what made her happy and content. On our excursions into the countryside, she enjoyed picking the grapes that remained in the vineyards and the mountain scenery, but overall she was not impressed with Switzerland and there was really only one place she wanted to go: Munkacs. So I thought, in my naiveté, perhaps it would be possible to take Mother to Munkacs for a few days. I would leave the children with Mark and take a long weekend and fly to wherever I needed to fly to and rent a car. At this point in time, I don't believe I had even located Munkacs on a map. I did know, however, that the borders had been redrawn after the war and unfortunately Munkacs was no longer part of Czechoslovakia, but rested within a remote corner of the Soviet Union. Of course I understood about the Soviet Bloc, but I did not understand about all the difficulties associated with traveling there. I called a travel agent and told him where I wanted to go and if he could help with the arrangements. Not too far into the conversation, he asked, "Are you Jewish?" and when I responded, he simply said, "No, no, no, you cannot go there," and abruptly hung up.

I did not pursue this matter anymore. The trip seemed overwhelming and cumbersome to arrange if not impossible. And of course it was impossible at this time. Foreigners were forbidden to travel to this area, it was most definitely off limits. Mom was disappointed, but there was nothing to be done about the situation and the idea was dropped.

We "made do" with Mother's vacation. We drove her around the quaint villages, we ate in the inviting restaurants, we ferried across idyllic lakes. Most people would have been thrilled to experience all these things. But Mother's capacity for joy was limited. The guilt she felt about my brother Michael's condition, his special needs, would not allow her to enjoy life. "How can I enjoy myself, when I have a son in those places?" she would say, for at this point Michael was living in an institution.

I was frustrated with her and our efforts to entertain her. She seemed happiest in my kitchen, baking her famous chocolate chip cookies or cooking a delicious Hungarian meal. When a friend once dropped by on a gorgeous summer day and saw Mother "slaving" over a steaming pot of stuffed cabbage she could not help but remark to me, "Why is your mother in the kitchen on a day like today?"

"Because that's what she likes to do," I replied.

* * *

The Soviet Union collapsed in 1990 and Mukacevo became part of an independent Ukraine; an unstable and dangerous Ukraine, if the stories were to be believed, but nevertheless out from under the clutches of the Soviets and now open to those who were brave enough to travel there.

We returned to the States that same summer and finally settled down determined not to move our family anymore. It would be many years later before the desire to see Munkacs became an overwhelming, driving force in my life.

14   Return to Chicago

I was determined to shorten our expatriate assignment and return to the United States to be with Mother. For as independent and strong a woman as she was, I knew she still struggled with loneliness and the lack of support of her family living so far away. I wanted to be near her as she aged and her health slowly started to fail. I saw signs of her decline on her last visits to Switzerland. She had developed problems with walking and balance and only at my insistence did she finally relent and use a cane. I persuaded Mark to curtail our time in "paradise," his description of our life in Geneva. I needed to assuage my guilt, return home, and help look after my mother.

And upon our return, Mother's anticipated health problems started almost immediately. Within a few months, she suffered a painful bout of shingles and this was to be the beginning of a long, protracted decline in her health. Eighteen years of frequent and intermittent periods of time spent in various hospitals and rehab facilities, so many times, it's impossible for me to remember them all. Numerous 911 emergency calls and hospital stays, some justly warranted as diabetes, congestive heart failure and other contributing ailments slowly, steadily wore Mother down.

Other times, it was fear. "It's so scary; they put you in the ground. They throw dirt on you," Mother would plaintively say, her voice quavering. Whenever Mother didn't feel well, it seemed a hospital stay would insure her immortality. She felt safe in the hospital. The doctors, whom she revered, took care of her.

Yet Mother kept on going. She rallied through all the hospitalizations and rehabilitation programs with sheer determination, driven by her strong will and overwhelming fear of death. The need to live for my brother's sake was powerful and she still oversaw his care, even when she could no longer bring him home every two months which she did until the age of eighty-nine.

* * *

Mother managed to live alone between her bouts of hospitalizations, but she was housebound for the last two years before she went to the nursing home. She had graduated from a cane to a walker, and because she had stubbornly refused to leave her walk-up apartment and move to an elevator building, it was the rare occasion when she would let us help her down the stairs for an outing.

She was able to live on her own with meals-on-wheels, and a geriatric home health care service where the doctors and nurses made house calls. There were two such services in the Chicago area, and one of them had "fired" Mother. The head doctor called me ranting one afternoon; he could no longer take care of Renee Stern. She was too difficult and demanding and he didn't have the patience that was required to continue caring for her.

I immediately contacted the other home health care service and signed Mother up. Then I informed her, "You have to behave yourself no matter what because we are running out of options." I was trying my best to have her live independently for as long as possible. It was what she desperately wanted.

After a stint in the hospital, until Mother felt strong enough to return to her apartment in the city, she would frequently recuperate for a few weeks at my home. Within a few days, Mother would head straight to my kitchen, rummage around in the refrigerator, and then begin to chop and sauté onions and potatoes as I watched incredulously. "It's do or die Bobbie," she responded to the look of amazement on my face.

On these visits, we would talk of many things. "I sent my parents packages but they were returned." I could hear the desolation in Mother's voice. The packages she sent her family were never received. The war broke out shortly after she left and the borders were sealed. The packages were returned unopened.

Only Florette, Uncle Irving's daughter and one of the oldest cousins, remembered getting a box from my grandparents before the war. She told me the story after Mother had died. Her memories were of glass jars filled with fruit preserves that had hardened from the long journey across the ocean. "It was good, I ate it like candy," Florette told me. I was envious.

* * *

Mother's pervasive preoccupation was with the past. She wasn't there in Europe to witness the catastrophe, but the emaciated and decaying corpses scattered on the ground, these terrible images revealed in the aftermath of the war, were ever present in her mind.

"One looked like my brother; I think I saw my brother laying there." She said this again and again through the years.

And perhaps it was one of her brothers. I never saw the picture she was referring to, but the Holocaust was well documented with photographs, there was no reason to doubt her. She could never be sure if it was Moishe Leibe or Joseph, but that the young dead man resembled her brother, haunted her to the end. I tried to imagine what it would be like, to carry an image like this of a beloved brother. One could only bear to remember rarely, and then repress the memory back into the compartment of pain where it would almost successfully remain for just a short space of time. That drawer would be locked until some trigger, perhaps a face, a smell, a landscape, would clutch open the drawer and claw out this painful memory. I could feel Mother's anguish as she remembered this picture, because after she would mention it, she let it go. She could not bear to dwell on the memory.

Again, she would question, "How could something like this happen in the twentieth century, in a modern world? No one cared, no one helped. Everyone turned their back on the Jews."

After the war, she was dismayed to discover the truth about President Roosevelt. The president, whom she had so admired and voted for, had known about the Jewish plight, and done nothing. He had closed the doors of America to the Jews; turned back the ships loaded with pleading desperate refugees and ignored requests to bomb the rail lines feeding into Auschwitz as well as the camp itself.

The Hungarian Jews were among the last Jews to be deported to Auschwitz, the last to needlessly die. "Hungarian sausage," it was a good joke among the German guards. My family was rounded up in May of 1944. Munkacs was liberated the following October. There was only a five month gap between one of the last deportations and liberation. If Roosevelt had destroyed the extermination center, perhaps my family would have survived. I would have known my grandparents.

* * *

Once I returned to the United States and settled down to raise my family, Mother would still express an interest in seeing

Munkacs again. But by this time, her desire was more of a dream. She knew in her heart she would never again see the Carpathian Mountains, the Latorica River, the Korzo. She was older then, in frail health and always in fear of dying.

I was busy raising a family in a new, larger house near the lake in Highland Park, and just happy to be rooted in a lovely community. We had traveled so much as expatriates that we were content to explore the United States on any vacations we took. The Berlin Wall fell and the Soviet Union collapsed, but it was only when I stopped by my old neighborhood to visit and saw Jerry once again that the idea of making an ancestral trip to Eastern Europe resurfaced.

Jerry had returned to Turka a few times by then. As soon as that area was out from under the Soviet domination he had felt it was safe to return. He even took his children back on one of the trips. This was when I started to understand that a trip to Ukraine was doable, it no longer felt so daunting and cumbersome. Jerry had visited Munkacs as well. He told me that the center of the city had been fixed up to make it more attractive and a wealthy Jewish businessman from New York had purchased the Hotel Star. This was an intriguing piece of information. The Hotel Star, the "Csillag," was the very same hotel Mother always spoke about; the big hotel located in the center of the city right on the Korzo where she worked. What did she say about the place, I'm no longer sure. I know that dignitaries, any important person visiting the town would usually stay there. I also remembered that the Hotel Star was considered to be an impressive place and the nicest hotel in the area. I later learned that, built in the 18th century, it had once been the residence of an Austro-Hungarian Count Earl von Shonbrun. It was converted into a hotel in 1920.

Because Jerry had safely returned to Ukraine, and more than once, I began thinking about making the trip myself. Of course, Jerry wasn't Jewish. He still had some friends and family in Turka who welcomed him. He could speak Russian and read Cyrillic. For me, it would not be so simple. There was no one left in my family, to my knowledge, living in Munkacs. I couldn't speak or read the language. Perhaps the people living in Mother's home, providing I could find it, would be hostile; worried I would try to reclaim my family's property. Was it safe? People said Ukraine was a dangerous, lawless place to travel. Police might be corrupt and one could not depend on them for help. A Jew traveling in these faraway places would be perceived as rich and vulnerable and subject to attack. All these risks surrounding an undertaking such as this whirled in my head.

And how does one actually, physically get there? Munkacs is located in the southwest corner of Ukraine, a remote area, which at the time seemed almost impossible to reach. What were the logistics of actually getting to this town? I would gaze at a map of this area but still could not figure out a solution. How did Jerry get there? He said something about flying to Vienna and then hiring a driver but some of the details went over my head. How would I communicate with the driver? Would he speak English?

It was too overwhelming, too daunting. My mother's health was rapidly declining, my children too young. Busy teaching and taking care of my family, it wasn't possible for me to make this trip yet. I couldn't leave my mother or my kids, and it would be many more years later before I would finally be able to do so.

15   The Final Good-Bye

Mark and I took a road trip to Charleston, South Carolina in June, 2007. We rented a condo for two weeks. With a few days driving time on either end, this was probably the longest vacation we had planned. For it seemed whenever we traveled anywhere, Mother would have an emergency and wind up in the hospital. I could never completely relax on these vacations for fear of getting "the call" as I so often did. It was into the second week of our stay in Charleston when I heard from Mother herself. In a panic, she was waiting for the ambulance once again to transport her from the nursing home to the hospital. She was sick, she couldn't eat, and so much worse was her palpable fear. I had been through this so many times before. This was routine. I go away on vacation, Mother goes to the hospital. More than a dozen years of this, I did not overly react. Before I left on the trip, I told her, "See you soon, see you in a few weeks."

"I hope so," she said as she always did, looking off through the large lobby window with that permanent look of misery carved into her face. After all, I never really thought my mother was going to die. I gave her my energy and kept her going for so long. Now I was worn out and so was she. Rationally of course, I knew in my heart that her death was inevitable. But somehow, I didn't really believe it and sometimes I still don't.

We drove back as quickly as we could when we realized after several phone calls from my sister, that this time things were truly serious. We arrived at the hospital, the afternoon of the 17th, and on June 18, 2007 Mother died at more than ninety-six and a half years old. She died after spending less than a week in the hospital surrounded by her children and grandchildren. She was old and sick and it was her time to leave this earth even though she would have wanted to go on forever. And right before she died, for just a moment she opened her eyes wide and looked at me. Her eyes were so blue. I had never noticed how blue her eyes were. Why, I wondered helplessly? Please give me another chance to really see you. Too late. Too late.

* * *

Her death is still so difficult for me. My mother was a part of my life for so long, I guess I couldn't imagine her not always being there. "The whole life is like a dream," she would say. Yes, I can see this for myself now. She was so afraid of death, we both tried together to stave it off as long as we could. And I was so cavalier about it. I would explain to her how everything that is born must die. Every bird, every flower. Eventually everything, everyone comes to an end. Everything is over. She didn't want to hear this. I became impatient, frustrated with her. This was ridiculous to me. One must accept death, it's part of life. But she would not, could not accept it.

"You'll feel differently when you're my age," she often said. I think she was right.

I tried spirituality. I suggested to her the possibility of another world where she would see her parents again. How wonderful that would be to embrace her family once again. She wasn't buying it.

"Are you kidding me, that's all a bunch of......." she rattled off something incomprehensible in Yiddish.

There was nothing I could say to make her feel better about the fact that her time was rapidly running out. But why didn't

I patiently humor her regardless?

She gazed out the window of her room at the nursing home. "Sometimes I cry," she whispered.

"Good-bye mother, I'll be back soon," I kissed her.

I could hardly breathe in that place. I needed to leave as quickly as possible. To go out into the sunshine, inhale the fresh air, meet my friends for coffee. I needed to feel alive.

What could I tell Mother after all? Yes Mother, you're going to live until two hundred like Sarah in the Bible (her role model for longevity). We'll find a wonderful new doctor who'll make you get better and back on your feet. He'll give you some new medications that will rejuvenate you and you'll be able to leave this smelly, horrible institution and live independently again. Why didn't I tell her what she wanted to hear? Console her, give her hope. This is my regret.

16   Summer of Sadness

The summer Mother died was consumed with everything one needs to do when a parent dies. After the funeral, there were forms to be filled out, calls to be made, sorting through personal possessions and then deciding what to do with them. What to save, give away, throw out; these were not easy tasks. Going into her apartment and seeing her furniture; where she sat, the shabby, worn recliner in front of the television, empty now. The old dented kitchen pots and pans...Why didn't I think to buy her a new set? Her mixing bowls and tea kettle, her clothes and shoes. The jumbled costume jewelry was nothing to fight over my sister and I both agreed, for Mother had no jewelry of any value apart from a few pieces she had given each of us many years ago.

Busy, busy with all these death related duties until they were finally finished. And then again: the realization, the emptiness, the void. Mother is really gone. No more multiple daily phone calls. No more obligatory visits to the nursing home. No more bills to pay. No more consultations with the doctor.

"Put him on the phone," she'd demand when she called his office. "I don't want to talk to a nurse, they don't know nottin".

No more errands to run for her, the list always the same: sugarless candy, cough drops and cookies. She needed cold cream and denture cleanser.

"Take care of your teeth Bobbie, these dammed dentures are a curse."

Sometimes she had a taste for "a little strip of lox" or a corned beef sandwich. When she died, there were three of them found partially eaten in the refrigerator at the nurses' station.

It was over, and I never expected it would be so hard for me. I, who never got along well with Mother, who found her at times to be cold and undemonstrative. I, who resented the attention she took from me and gave to my brother whose care she was consumed with; I was the proverbial middle child, lost and neglected somewhere in the midst of my family.

People told me it takes a year after losing a parent to feel oneself again. It's been two years now as I'm writing this, and yes I am a bit better than I was but I still miss her so much. And I still can't believe she's gone. I, who was so rational and dismissive about dying; this is my punishment, for now I am as disbelieving and in denial of death as was Mother.

Her old neighborhood, her tired apartment; we fortunately sold it almost immediately it went on the market despite my sister's cries, "We'll never sell this place."

The neighbors are still there. Lonely, eccentric Martha who lived next door; in her late 60's she still wore a long dyed black pony tail and a ton of makeup. Her lips colored bright red, her favorite color; it was the same color of her carpet and matching drapes. She often depended on my mother for a hot home cooked meal.

The Lebanese family who lived in the apartment below was always kind, bringing Mother food and sharing their barbecue dinners in the summer. When she was still able, they occasionally drove her to the facility miles away where Michael lived and helped bring him home for the weekend.

But I cannot bring myself to go there to stop in and say hello, especially in the summer, when I visited more frequently and we would sit and gossip on the back porch to pass the time. And the air was sweet with a soft wind on a sunny day. No, I cannot go back.

* * *

I honored my mother's memory at her funeral with a short speech. I wanted those in the audience who knew me and had so often listened to me complain about Mother that I did indeed love her very much. And even though my mother was not perfect, she still had so many wonderful qualities that needed to be recognized. She helped me with the children and she was there for me when I needed her most. A kindhearted woman who adored and appreciated nature, she once saved a fly from drowning in a bucket of water. She couldn't bear to see it struggle and fight for its life, she quickly scooped it out and put it in the sun to dry and then watched it fly away.

In my speech, I spoke about how my mother had longed to return for a visit to Mukacevo but unfortunately she was never able to make this trip. I promised to make the trip for her, and the following year was spent in trying to figure out exactly how to do that.

17 Making Plans

I realized a trip to Ukraine was now possible. Daniel Mendelsohn, author of *The Lost* and Howard Reich, who wrote *The First and Final Nightmare of Sonia Reich* had both made trips similar to the one I wanted to make and survived to write about their experiences. I would do the same.

In the fall, following Mother's death and after her affairs were settled, I set myself the task of returning to Mukacevo. I was driven. I was compelled. I had to make this trip and soon. Mark and I were still young and healthy, but there was a feeling of urgency for me. Now was the time to make this trip while it was still possible for us, before it was too late. Our children were grown and self-sufficient, and although Sandy our aged yellow Labrador retriever had slowed down somewhat, she was still healthy as well.

The logistics of the trip baffled me. Mukacevo, located in the southwest corner of what is now Ukraine, is a remote area tucked away in a valley at the foot of the Carpathian Mountains. It is far from any major Ukrainian airport and Mark voiced his

concerns about the caliber and quality of the planes and crew that

flew to and from those places.

Stories began to surface about crazy drivers and cars

being stopped at gunpoint, people robbed of their valuables or

physically harmed, corrupt police. It all sounded very scary but I

was not deterred. I made many inquiries, a few false starts and

after much searching of various tour groups, I found our guide,

Alex Dunai. He was the same Ukrainian guide that Daniel

Mendelsohn had used for his travels and his name seemed to

surface everywhere I turned. He was recommended as a well-

educated, knowledgeable man, someone who was familiar with

Mukacevo, who could be trusted to drive, protect and translate for

us while we explored Mother's town. Looking on the map, I noticed

Mukacevo was not far from the Hungarian border, just 250 miles

east of Budapest. Crossing the border always seemed so

formidable to me, but now Alex agreed to pick us up in Budapest,

facilitate the border crossing and drive us into Ukraine. Everything

came together for me at this point. I had a respected guide and a

city I felt safe flying in and out of. My father was from

Szekesfehervar, a town located 40 miles southwest from

Budapest. My paternal grandfather had been a prominent

illustrator and artist, perhaps we would be able to find some

information about him or locate some of his artwork. The prospect

of this impending adventure and all its' possibilities, all the things I

might see or discover was thrilling. I couldn't ever remember being

so excited. My expectations were high, yet somehow I knew in my

heart, I would not be disappointed.

18 Preparations for Travel

Long before we left for Europe, I had read that medication to prevent typhoid fever should be taken when traveling in Ukraine. I was hesitant about taking the pills, but Mark, who had taken a multitude of vaccinations and tablets before his extensive international travels, was not intimidated.

"Better take the pills, than risk contracting typhoid," he said.

Mother had almost died from typhus, another grave disease that raged through Eastern Europe in 1918. At seven years old, she lay in bed delirious with fever but still somehow able to hear the doctor from the next room tell her mother that she would not make it through the night. Well of course she made it through that night, and many more years of nights, but she always blamed her thin hair on the illness.

She mourned her lost hair, "It was from the high fever," she always said, and it never grew back to its original fullness. Still it was a lovely, wavy, deep auburn. Titian, she called this color.

So we armed ourselves with our typhoid pills taken at the eleventh hour and hepatitis vaccinations, antibiotics and a myriad of other over the counter drugs. Health insurance was another consideration. What if something happened to us while we were traveling in Ukraine, a car accident or the onset of a sudden serious medical problem? After some investigation, Mark bought us a temporary health insurance policy that provided coverage for our trip and that also included necessary medical evacuation. This was the type of insurance that was carried by many corporate employees who traveled internationally to countries that could not be counted on to provide the best of health care. Over the years, he had heard the scary stories of colleagues who had had some sort of medical emergency and would have fared better if they had been flown out of the country. The man who thought he was having a heart attack while traveling on business in China was a salient tale. While suffering from chest pains, he had to walk up six flights of stairs to the emergency room. Fortunately, it was just indigestion.

Then there was the question of what clothes to bring on the trip. We wanted to travel light and look inconspicuous although everyone said it would be impossible to do.

"Americans can be spotted from a mile away no matter how shabbily they dress," people warned us.

I did not want to stand out from the crowd and so we chose a few articles of old, drab clothes to take. We purchased some lightweight easy-care clothes made from material that could be washed and dried quickly on the road. Mark hesitated about a dull gray green raincoat that made his skin look a sickly green.

"Buy it," I said. "You don't want to look good where we're going." I took no expensive jewelry apart from wearing my plain gold wedding band and a small pair of simple gold earrings.

While at work, I heard a horror story from one of the teachers. A student of hers returned to Ukraine for a visit. She was intent on showing off to her friends how she had fared so well in the U.S., so she traveled back wearing expensive jewelry. It was promptly removed at gunpoint by a cabdriver who picked her up from the airport. He forced her to remove all her clothes and then left her naked in a wooded area. Fortunately she escaped with her life, but I can't understand why she did not know better than to attract attention to herself in this manner. Mark and I were not going to make this mistake. We were not traveling to Eastern Europe to impress anyone. We were going on an adventure, to discover my roots, and to look for what might remain of the world my mother had left behind.

* * *

A week before our departure, our dog Sandy's health suddenly started to deteriorate. At fourteen years old she limped painfully and with labored breathing, she had recently collapsed on a walk. Then she lost interest in food. Mark and I wanted to put an end to her suffering, but our son Matt insisted we give Sandy another chance with a new medication the vet suggested might help. He was in denial, struggling with the inevitable loss of his beloved dog, yet he was responsible. Matt assured us he would take care of and do what was necessary with our family pet.

19   A Week in Budapest

We arrived in London at midnight and stayed at a hotel near the airport. This allowed us to get some rest and reduce the jet lag from a long, tiring flight before beginning our adventure. The next morning, August 29, we flew to Budapest.

My first impression on the bus to our hotel was not so favorable. The buildings on the outskirts of the city were drab, grim and covered with graffiti, but as we got closer to the center of the city, my opinion of Budapest improved. Our hotel, Le Meridian was lovely. Part of the French chain, it was small, intimate and beautifully furnished. The staff was friendly and very helpful with all our questions about our new and strange surroundings.

I had spent a few months before our trip teaching myself Hungarian. I bought language tapes and from those I managed to learn a few necessary phrases: "koszoszom," thank you; "szia" hi; "bocsanat," sorry. I loved it. I loved hearing Hungarian again and I loved that I could speak it, if only just a few phrases. My parents never taught us the language. My mother was discouraged from speaking Hungarian to us. "Don't you want the children to have friends, people will think they're greenhorns," her family said. We should only speak English so we could be real Americans, have American friends, be part of the American dream. She did not take the opportunity nor see the advantage of teaching us to be bi-lingual.

As we explored the city, I struggled with the language and the old resentment resurfaced. It would have been easy for our parents to teach us Hungarian, so wonderful and advantageous to speak another language fluently. Hungarian is one of the most difficult languages to learn, and there are only eleven million speakers in the world. I tried to let it go. My parents were gone, they did what they thought was right at the time. But, oh the language! How it brought me back to my youth and I longed to communicate with those around me. The frustration, yes, I too am Hungarian.

I chose Budapest for two reasons. One was the proximity to Mukacevo, an easy four hour drive east. After extensive research, I found this was often a convenient starting point where my guide picked up his clients. But the foremost reason I chose

Budapest was the close proximity to my father's town. In 1911, Gyorgy Grynzpan was born in Szekesfehervar, just a little more than an hour train ride from the big city. It would make a wonderful day trip where we could explore the place where father grew up and studied to be an artist.

My paternal grandfather was a prominent political cartoonist and illustrator before the war. He divorced my grandmother when my father was very young and then abandoned his family. My father had dim recollections of visiting with his dad a few times. Only once he took him to a circus. His father tossed him aside, pursued his career, and went about the business of becoming a well-known and respected graphic artist. Born Eugene Grynzpan, he became Tabor Jeno or Janos.

The first thing on our agenda was to visit the Szechenyi library located in the castle complex up on Buda Hill. Before the trip, I had researched and found a cartoonist, a Mr. Joe Beckesi, whom I contacted via the internet. I asked him if perhaps he might have heard of my grandfather whom I only knew as Eugene or Eugenio Tabor. Eugenio was the name he used while he lived in Buenos Aires, the city where he escaped to during the war.

Beckesi wrote me back. There was information about Tabor Jeno in the national library and it was available to the public. I was excited to discover that Jeno was the name he used in Europe; this was one of the more useful pieces of information I learned.

* * *

Mark and I set out for Castle Hill on a beautiful, warm and sunny morning. It was the day after our arrival in Budapest and as we walked across the Chain bridge and up the hill, I was filled with anticipation. The library was deserted and quiet so the two librarians we found sitting idle at their desk seemed delighted to help us; to have something interesting and useful to do. They spoke no English but between my rudimentary Hungarian and another librarian they found who did speak some English and could translate, we were able to explain what we were looking for. They began to research on their computers and after a few attempts they found several entries for Tabor Jeno. One was an illustration within a book which they brought to us and Mark quickly took a picture of it. But the big find was the archival collection. There were several original pieces of artwork in their archives that could only be viewed at the library but not removed.

They were part of the library's permanent collection. This news was very exciting for both of us and we were anxious to see the artwork, but we were to be kept waiting. For in Hungary, there is still a plodding bureaucracy, an ever present holdover from the Soviet period. It was Saturday and the archives were closed. We had to fill out forms and requisition the artwork; it would be not be available for viewing until later in the week when the library would reopen. We had no choice but to follow their procedures and expectantly wait the few days while we continued to explore Budapest.

For the next few days, we wandered through the center of the city which is situated on both sides of the Danube River. The weather was hot, almost too warm for sightseeing, but I did not complain. We were blessed with clear sunny skies and it made everything much brighter and more exciting.

The art museum on Buda Hill held many works of the famous Hungarian genre painter Munkascy Mihail. In 1844, he was born to German parents in Munkacs, and at that time it was common for people to take the name of their birthplace and make it their own. His paintings are very dark, rendered in somber tones of black and brown; pastoral landscapes and scenes of people going about their everyday life. One sees peasants and poor people shopping in the markets, walking in the streets and working in their homes. Sometimes it was difficult to distinguish the figures in the foreground from those in the background in these old faded canvasses done by Munkacsy, a famous artist born in Mother's town. Perhaps some of these landscapes were of the same scenery Mother had known.

The annual Jewish festival was in progress and it was a fortunate coincidence for us. In the evening we attended a klezmer concert at the largest synagogue in Europe, the Dohany synagogue, where I sat sobbing to the sounds of the haunting melodies. During the day we toured the synagogue, and explored its cemetery where two thousand Jews from the ghetto are buried. We saw *The Tree of Life* by Imre Varga, the silvery metal sculpture in the shape of a weeping willow. It's silvery metal leaves are each inscribed with the name of a person who was murdered by the Nazis.

And there in the courtyard we found a plaque, a tribute to Angelo Roncalli, Pope John Paul XXIII, the benevolent, ecumenical pope who had saved Jews during the war. My father had painted his portrait in the 1960's; a large, beautiful portrait but not very marketable. The painting floated around our family for years, traveling from my sister's storage locker to my basement. No one knew what to do with it. I wasn't comfortable hanging this large life-like picture, yet I was reluctant to part with a piece of art my father had created. So when I saw the tribute to this pope, I decided that because he had made the effort to save Jews during the war, a fact I had not known before, the portrait would hang in my home after all.

* * *

We stopped to chat with one of the synagogue's employees in its small museum. His name was Joseph, an elderly gentleman sitting on a stool, whom I assumed was there as "security" watching the tourists as they looked at the exhibits. He was friendly, his English was good, and he told us about the antisemitism that still existed in Hungary. "People blame the Jews for the poor economy. This is how it started, first the talk and then Auschwitz."

Mark mentioned our plans to cross the Hungarian border, enter Ukraine, and visit Munkacs. Suddenly his face darkened. "Be careful, be very careful. The people are even poorer there, there's crime," he warned.

"We're going with a guide, an experienced guide. He's going to drive us and take care of us," I replied.

"Still, be very careful," he repeated.

And so, with a few words, Joseph reinforced my nervousness and misgivings, feelings I had, but was trying to repress as the day of our departure for Ukraine drew closer.

After we left the museum, I adamantly told Mark not to tell anyone else where we were going. "I don't want to hear about the dangers of going into Ukraine. I want to go. I have to go. I'm determined to see Mother's town and I'm going no matter what anyone says."

At this time, there was strife in the separatist region of South Ossetia, a part of Georgia which borders Ukraine and Russia. The border dispute threatened to spill over into Ukraine and the Russians were posturing and positioning tanks. The conflict was featured on the news every night and there was much tension in that area of the world. Our son Matthew was worried. He phoned with his fears about our trip and also gave us unwelcome updates on our dying dog. I started to have serious misgivings and at one point my nerves bested me. I told Mark to call Alex and tell him not to meet us on Saturday. In my heart, I was not serious. I wanted Mark to dissuade me from changing our plans.

"It's too late, we're going, the die is cast," he said as he tried on the contraption he had bought to conceal his money and documents beneath his clothes. And he was right. I knew he was right. This was an adventure and I was scared, but I was thrilled at the same time.

We spent the remaining days in Budapest continuing to explore the city, anxiously awaiting Saturday and what the day would hold for us.

The days passed quickly. On Wednesday, we took the train to Szekesfehervar and walked in my father's town. Hot again, the sun baked the cobbled streets as we wandered. It was several blocks from the train station to the center of town. A charming old city filled with Roman ruins, flowers and all types of trees. I didn't have any addresses and I didn't know where my father's house had been. His cousin Eva said it no longer existed. But still I had to go there, to at least see the city where father was born and spent his youth. We walked around in the heat, ate chicken paprikash for lunch at a quaint outdoor restaurant, for it seems Hungarians eat the same heavy food all year, and took a late afternoon train back to Budapest.

Before our trip, I read Ronald Zweig's book, *The Gold Train,* which described in detail the plunder of the Hungarian Jewish property and the deportations. Szekesfehervar was the town where the Gestapo set up their headquarters. Many of the wealthy Jews were taken there and tortured into revealing where they had hidden their riches before they were put on the trains for Auschwitz. By the time they arrived at the camps, they were among those in the worst condition. Half dead from their beatings in Hungary, they were immediately put to death. As I looked out the train window watching the fields pass, I reflected on my day with mixed emotions. Excited to see my father's town that seemed so idyllic, I could see at the same time all the horrors that took place there.

Remarkably, a few of my father's first cousins are still alive. Before the trip, I had located Eva Katzman, now in her mid 80's living in Florida. She freely gave me a brief history of what happened to her and other members of my father's family when they were deported from Szekesfehervar. She told me of the train ride. She was with her mother Roza Brown, my paternal grandmother's sister, another Aunt Mulvina and other family members. When they arrived in Auschwitz, she saw the infamous Dr. Mengele. Her head was shaved. Her mother and her vowed to stay together and die together if they must. She told me this story in nervous fits and starts. I had only the dimmest recollection of meeting Eva when I was a little girl living in New York. She had a dark olive complexion, was very beautiful, and she was just a teenager in 1944.

Eva told me about her mother Roza whom I also vaguely

remembered from our years of living in New York. She was my grandmother's sister and whenever we visited her we would eat from her bowl of hard candy. There was a funny story that drifted through our family for years, and it came to be known as "Roza Nani and the hard candy." I can no longer remember the details, but it was something to do with her wanting to hoard and hide the candy for her own grandchildren. She begrudgingly allowed us a few pieces. She too was dark complexioned but heavy, and a widow who had lost her husband in the camps.

Within a year after my father's mother Julia died, her sister Roza married my step-grandfather, another Eugene, and this caused a family rift. My father and Roza's son, his cousin Steve, were close, but there were hard feelings on both sides of the family after the marriage. My father did not receive his mother's life insurance policy she intended for him. Instead, it went to the newlyweds. I believe this was the reason my family decided to leave New York.

From Eva, I learned Roza committed suicide a few years ago. She jumped from a window in her apartment. Eva didn't know why, apart from the obvious: she was depressed. Eva mentioned some family issues, but perhaps in addition to everything else she had to deal with in life, her struggle with the past had stolen her strength and desire to continue living.

Another dim memory, Mother is talking about Eva. She was subjected to experiments in the camps. The doctors tried to sterilize her but failed. Shortly after the war, she married and gave birth to two children.

* * *

We explored Budapest in the remaining days. The weather continued to be delightful, warm and sunny. We walked everywhere, up the lovely, leafy Andrassy Ut, all the way to Heros Square and on to Varosliget, the city park. It was an oasis in the heart of the city with beautiful old buildings of classic and neoclassic architecture, large leafy plane trees, a zoo, a small circular pond surrounded with benches, and a permanent circus. This must be the circus where Grandfather took my father when he was very young. It was one of the few memories Dad had of spending time with his father before the man completely disappeared from his life.

Shabby and tired looking, like many parts of Budapest, the park's beauty haunted me. I could clearly see the ghosts of the people that once strolled there, around the pond and through the park: where once there were so many Jewish faces, now there were none. The vibrancy and energy Jewish people can bring to a society were gone.

We left the park, and braving the challenge of a strange transportation system, rode the subway to the antique district located on Falk Miksa Utca where lush shady trees lined the streets. We searched through the shops looking for any Tabor art but turned up nothing. And just a few blocks from this quiet beauty, along the Danube River were the *Danube Shoes*. This is the memorial to the Jews who were murdered by the Hungarian Fascists, the Arrow Cross. The Jewish people were taken down to the river and shot at the water's edge; their bodies tumbled into the Danube. There were simple rows of bronzed shoes; womens' shoes, men's shoes, children's shoes, baby shoes. The hatred and horror did not discriminate. Jews of every age did not escape this hell.

More stories about Father's family came back to me. Eva told me about Hugo, my father's favorite uncle whom he loved so much. Father always believed Hugo was shot and killed as he was running to a train. But Eva told me what really happened. After the war ended, Hugo returned to his apartment in Budapest and it was there that the Arrow Cross murdered him. Even though the war was officially over, the chaos and mob rule continued until the Allies could restore order. Gangs of murderous Arrow Cross roamed the streets and killed as many Jews as they could. A week later, Hugo's gentile wife hung herself.

Within the last few years, I learned another family story about Moti, my cousin Ruth's Hungarian husband. Today they live in Tel Aviv together. In 1944, Moti was six years old living in Budapest with his parents, two sisters and another brother. The children were separated from their parents and each other, and then given to gentile families who were paid to protect them. Moti's "family" took the money and threw him on the street. At six years old, he roamed Budapest alone until a policeman scooped him up off the street and took him to a Jewish orphanage. At the end of the war he was sent to a displaced person's camp in France where he found his older brother. Together they made their way to Israel where he was reunited with his family. Remarkably, they had all survived; his parents and his four siblings. Several years later Mark and I would travel to Israel where we had the opportunity to meet many members of this fortunate family.

20 Friday, September 5

This was our last day in Budapest until we planned to return on the 11th. We were busy shopping for souvenirs. Before we left for Europe, one of my friends mentioned a fabulous skin cream her Hungarian hairstylist always brings back from her frequent trips to Budapest.

"Helia D is the name," my friend told me.

And so I excitedly bought several jars for myself, family and friends.

We bought paprika from the Great Market Hall, a vast two story indoor market filled with everything Hungarian; all types of meat and sausage, cheeses, spices, colorful displays of fruits and vegetables. Upstairs, there was stall after stall of souvenirs; embroidered aprons and tablecloths. Steam tables served the hot, heavy Hungarian food even though it was more than 80 degrees outside.

We went to a book store where we found Hungarian history books. We stopped at a small market and stocked up on bottled water, fruit and snacks for our trip, for we were leaving for Mukacevo the next morning. We took a boat ride down the Danube and then in the afternoon we returned to the library to view my grandfather's art.

There in a small musty room, the archives, the librarian presented us with an old manila folder filled with Tabor Jeno's artwork; a few dozen caricatures drawn in pencil on aged yellowing paper. All the men and one woman had signed their portraits. It was thrilling to touch, to view. Several of the caricatures were dated; the latest was 1936 of an Olympian athlete in Berlin. The earliest drawing dated as far back as 1915. We had no idea who most of these people in the pictures were, but it appeared they all had Hungarian names. For a small fee, it was our good fortune the librarians were willing and able to scan the artwork for us on a DVD.

It was later, upon our return to the United States, when I could research the signatures on the internet, that I discovered these people were all prominent: writers, artists, politicians, and even the famous actress, Vilma Banky, who made movies with

Rudolf Valentino.

Self portrait

* * *

During the week, our son Matthew called us with news

about our ailing dog Sandy. We had spent a wonderful week in

Budapest. We found my grandfather's artwork, we visited the town where my father was born, listened to haunting klezmer music in the Dohany Synagogue, discovered a skin cream I fooled myself into believing was my mother's formula. All these amazing experiences, and yet our pet's looming death cast a pall on our last day.

I loved Sandy and cared for her although it had not been easy. I broke an ankle walking that dog. She was haughty, regal and independent; a dog that had bitten three people over the years, not the gentle, yellow Labrador retriever we thought we had chosen when my children picked her from her litter. "We got the wrong dog," my older daughter Hedy would remark. The other, more docile female puppy was being cuddled by the owner's son as my family drove away with our new frisky pet. If I petted Sandy, she would shrug away from my hand and take three steps backward. She was not a needy dog. Food, walks, playing catch, those were her pleasures. As for people, yes she did like us I guess, but more from a distance and on her own terms.

I was torn between grieving for Sandy and continuing to revel in the joy of having my lifetime dream come true. To see my parent's birthplace and discover my roots was an experience I had longed for. So I chose the latter. I consoled myself in knowing we gave Sandy a good home. "We gave her a name," my daughter said. She was loved, sheltered and doted on for fourteen years. She lived to be an old lady; a sick, frail old lady who stopped eating and was in a lot of pain. She could no longer eat, get up or walk. It was time to let her go.

21 Munkacs

September 6 finally arrived, the day we would drive to Mukacevo. I was a bundle of nerves, filled with anticipation and excitement. The South Ossetian conflict worsened and dominated the news. I didn't quite understand everything about this border dispute between Georgia and Russia, but the Russians were threatening to invade Ukraine. People's warnings, Matthew's fears, I squelched them all as we hurriedly ate breakfast and finished packing our suitcases. We had agreed to meet Alex at 10:00 in the morning downstairs in the hotel lobby. Even though *we* hadn't spoken in a few weeks, I never doubted that he would be there. From our correspondence and all the positive recommendations, I had every confidence Alex was reliable, so when Alex did not show up promptly at 10:00 a.m., I was not concerned. After waiting for ten minutes, Mark was impatient and insisted I call him on his cell phone.

Alex answered immediately. He was stuck in traffic and

would arrive momentarily which he did within a few minutes. He entered the small lobby and walked over to the chairs where we were sitting. He never glanced around; it was as if he knew us. It's said that no matter how hard one tries to blend in with the natives, wears the oldest, crummiest clothes which is about all we had packed, one is still noticeably American.

I had described us to Alex. I, with my curly red hair and Mark who is 6'4", he couldn't miss us. But what about Alex? How would I know him? For months I had tried to imagine Alex. There was no real description of him in Daniel Mendelsohn's book apart from referring to Alex as large. Somehow, in my mind, I thought large meant tall. Mark teased me. He said I was fantasizing about Alex, picturing him to look like the actor, Nick Nolte. It was not far from the truth. A cross between Nick Nolte and Viggo Mortenson is whom I imagined; a tall man, lean with angular features, icy blue eyes, close cropped hair and a day's beard, a man with a serious demeanor dressed in a black leather jacket.

So when we met Alex, I do believe my mouth did open and my jaw did drop in disbelief. My fantasy man evaporated. Alex's largeness was not in his height but in his girth; husky with a large face, two chins and a wide neck. It was a wrestler's body we later learned. He wore Bermuda shorts, a T-shirt and sneakers. After the initial surprise at Alex's appearance, I relaxed. For Alex was friendly and affable and put us totally at ease. He expressed surprise at our luggage, just one small carry-on suitcase for each of us, as he quickly stowed the bags in the trunk of his car.

We left Budapest in his blue VW Passat station wagon and started driving east towards the Hungarian border. I was impressed with the roads, for they were new and in great condition. The city soon turned into countryside and it was beautiful. The Hungarian plains are rich agricultural land and we saw corn crops, apple orchards and sunflower fields. It looked like Iowa, Nebraska, sections of Pennsylvania. Parts of the landscape reminded me of the countryside near Lyon France; tall, thin leafy trees shadowed and lined the roads that became narrow at one point.

Alex drove fast, 100 miles an hour fast. At one point I couldn't help myself and mentioned something about his excessive speed and suggested he might slow down a tad.

"Relax," he said. "I love life, I love my family, you'll be fine."

And so I would be fine, I told myself, for I wasn't about to argue with a Ukrainian wrestler in the middle of the Hungarian countryside. Resignedly, I put myself in Alex's big, beefy hands and turned my face towards the window where I soaked in the scenery and could not see the speedometer. Fortunately, I was sitting in the back seat, so the sense of speed and danger were somewhat mitigated. Mark, however, being up front in the passenger's seat, did not have this small comfort. He sat stoically with his chin in hand saying nothing in regard to Alex's driving, as he continued to drive as if he was a participant in a video game. Passing cars on a two lane road, barely missing the oncoming traffic, Alex whizzed across the Hungarian highways playing music and eating sunflower seeds.

Alex, who lived in Lvov, was not just a driver, he was an intelligent, educated man who had been a history major at the university and was very knowledgeable about the area. As he drove along, we discussed Ukraine's complicated history. Mukacevo is located in a region that was called Carpathian Ruthenia and is still referred to as Transcarpathia or Subcarpathia. At the end of World War I and the dissolution of the

Austro-Hungarian Empire, this largely Hungarian-speaking area was ceded to Czechoslovakia under the Treaty of Trianon. In 1938, under the Vienna Award, Hitler allowed the Hungarians to annex this region until the end of World War II. It then became part of the Soviet Union until it's collapse in 1990. Now Mukacevo is part of an independent Ukraine. Someone jokingly wrote, "I've lived in Czechoslovakia, Hungary, Russia and Ukraine and I've never left Munkacs".

The four-hour drive flew by, and soon we were nervously approaching the border. We were leaving Hungary behind, crossing over into the border town of Chop, and entering Ukraine; a strange country that held a host of negative associations for us. A place we had heard and read about, but had not yet dared to visit. The Germans' eager, sadistic accomplices, the Ukrainians, it was said, "were the worst".

I had heard the stories of other ethnic groups in that area and from that time of war. The Hungarians, the Latvians, the Lithuanians, certainly the Poles. The list goes on and on. So how is it possible that everyone was "the worst?" Did the war uncover the bestiality in people? Was all the repressed, smoldering hatred of the Jews unleashed because it was sanctioned, because it was okay?

Some said, "Why ask where was God, where was man?"

As I sat silent and scared, the Ukrainian border guards looked over our papers and passports. Alex quickly helped us fill out some forms and after about forty-five minutes we were no longer in Hungary but speeding faster than before in Ukraine.

Immediately I could see the difference from Hungary. The roads were in much need of repair. The small poor houses were even poorer looking than those we had seen. But somehow, this scene, this landscape was what I had imagined. And what struck me were the flowers; all kinds, a profusion of flowers growing in the gardens of these small homes. My mother had loved flowers and I could now see why. She grew up in a place where people were poor, yet they appreciated the wonders of nature. The beauty and intricacy of flowers gave my mother joy. They brightened up her difficult life. When she worked in the yard, planting seeds and weeding for a few hours, she could forget her problems for awhile. This was her therapy, losing herself and working hard in the garden. There were no antidepressants or psychologists for Mother. And she was always so thrilled, when from the seeds, the flowers finally bloomed.

In less than an hour Alex announced we were on the outskirts of Mukacevo, and in a short time we entered the city. We went directly to check in at the Hotel Star, the Csillag, as it was called in Hungarian. It was 3:00 in the afternoon, a beautiful, warm, sunny day and I was overwhelmed with emotion. We were staying at the hotel Mother had spoken about my whole life; once the home of an aristocrat, now a small and charming hotel. The outside was painted shades of bright yellow and there, on the top of a turret, was a star with six points, the Star of David! Perhaps, it was the Jewish owner's way of showing this part of the world, that yes, some of us Jews did survive and live to prosper.

Inside, the lobby's furnishings appeared to be dated, yet everything was gleaming. The original mahogany reception desk, the dark wood banisters and steps of the staircase, it was all clean and polished.

Our suite was not grand compared to western standards, but it was clean and comfortable with a television that worked well and a small refrigerator to keep our water bottles cold. Alex recommended we drink only bottled water in Ukraine so we had bought a supply in Budapest. The one problem with our room was the stench from the bathroom. Stench is the only word that can describe the horrid smell that apparently came from the sewer system. Nothing to be done about it, except to keep the bathroom door closed at all times, and not linger too long when using the facilities. But the view from the room was lovely. The window opened up over the rooftops of the city and in the distance rose the steeple of the Catholic church.

We agreed to meet Alex for dinner after we had rested in our room for a few hours. Alex, happy to relax as well, was staying in the room next door to us. I'm not sure if that was deliberate, but it was a comfort. I know Alex felt responsible, was responsible, for our safety. I did not feel threatened but we were in a strange country where English speakers were few. This wasn't a tourist area. We could neither speak nor read the language. We needed Alex to take care of us, and that he did very well. Later in the trip, he would pull out a large sharp knife to cut something for me. I wondered then if he carried a small arsenal of weapons to protect his clients. Corruption, kidnapping, robbery, murder; these were all the very real possibilities. I felt that Alex was well prepared for them, even though be wasn't talking about it.

Later in the afternoon we met Alex downstairs in the lobby. It was still light, so we decided to take a stroll around the downtown before eating. This was the Korzo, the main street Mother had reminisced about so often. What a pleasant surprise. Jerry had mentioned that the downtown had been spruced up, and it was true. The buildings were charming, clean and freshly painted in colorful pastels of pink, tan and salmon. Across the street from the yellow Hotel Star was the Varoshaza, the town hall, painted in shades of bright blue green.

The center of the street was divided by a boulevard planted with a variety of evergreen trees. Most of the buildings and store fronts had containers filled with flowers. These were Munkacs' original buildings, the same buildings that stood when Mother strolled in its old cobbled streets. The Soviets had built a few utilitarian structures, but overall everything seemed to have remained the same. The city was not destroyed during the war and so it stayed, largely untouched through the years. Under the Soviets the city languished in a state of disrepair, but after the system's collapse, it was evident that the Ukrainians had made an effort to restore at least a few of the main streets in the downtown area.

It was late afternoon and there were few people about, when Alex suddenly pointed out a small family walking in front of us; a slight, disheveled dark complexioned mother pushing a baby in a carriage, another little girl of five or six years walking beside her. "Those are gypsies, go ahead take their picture," Alex said.

I did take their picture and the little girl became upset and then I felt an immediate regret. The gypsies, the Cygany, the disenfranchised Roma who live on the margins of society. How often my mother had spoken about the mysterious gypsies. No one knew exactly from where they originated; some believed they had migrated from India. They were a nomadic people who lived an unconventional lifestyle. Men and women often lived together without marriage, something unheard of in Mother's community. It was said there were unsavory types among the gypsies, murderers and thieves, yet many were talented musicians who performed at Jewish weddings.

We stopped for dinner at a small outdoor restaurant

around the corner from the Hotel Star, and had a delicious meal of veal steak, roasted potatoes and fresh tomatoes. During dinner, we talked over our plans for the next day. Mark and I decided to slow down the pace. We had done a lot of chasing in Budapest, cramming each day with so many activities, and still we were unable to see everything we wanted to see. We wanted to explore Munkacs in a more leisurely way. I had a list of things I wanted to see and do and after agonizing about how much time I should spend in Ukraine, we had decided to allow for an extra day.

Hedy had persuaded us. "Perhaps you'll meet someone from the past and you'll want to spend more time," she said.

Not likely, I thought, for everyone is gone now. But still, it was my mother's town and the odds were that I would not return for a long time, if ever. I did not want to rush. I wanted to know I had enough time to see and do everything I had planned for. When we finished dinner, we agreed to meet Alex for breakfast the next morning at 9 a.m. in the hotel's restaurant. After breakfast, we were going to tackle the number one priority on my list: finding Mother's house.

* * *

Later that night, in our hotel room, we learned Sandy was gone. Matt and Hedy phoned a veterinarian who agreed to euthanize her at home as she lay outside on our front lawn, where she could no longer get up to walk or eat. There was something poignant about losing our family pet the same day we arrived in Munkacs. Melancholy and disquiet mixed in with the emotions of the day, it was a loss for our family. I knew I would feel her absence when we returned home, so I decided to try and put her death out of my mind for the remainder of our trip.

The following day when Alex heard the news, he tried to appear appropriately sympathetic. It was a mediocre acting job.

"In Ukraine a dog is a dog and a person is a person." Later, as we stood outside of the hotel, Alex pointed to the ground. "This earth, right here, is soaked with blood."

The grief that followed losing a pet was an emotion Alex felt should be reserved for human suffering.

22 Gypsy Music Street

In the morning, as we ate breakfast I observed the Hotel Star's restaurant. It was a grand and ornate room decorated with heavy red velvet drapes tied back to frame the large windows. There were white linen tablecloths and fine silverware and china plates, and we were the only people in the room. The full breakfast was delicious and was included with the price of our room. We enjoyed omelets and an assortment of cold cuts, but interestingly we were served only one cup of coffee. The second cup of coffee cost extra, and it seemed to be an inconvenience for the waiter when we made the request as he scurried off to the kitchen. Coffee must be expensive in Ukraine.

After breakfast, we walked across the street and down the Korzo to a small bookstore where Alex bought a map of Munkacs. He stopped an elderly man on the street and asked him if he knew the location of Zenez Ut, Music Street. As the man gesticulated and spoke to Alex in Ukrainian, I could sense from their conversation it was not far. How could it be far when Mother walked to and from work? When she walked home for lunch? I knew her home had to be nearby.

Alex quickly found the street on the map and then we began to walk. Up the Korzo and around the corner, immediately the streets became more tired looking. Everywhere, the sidewalks were cracked and worn, the rounded ancient cobblestones whittled smooth. These were the very same worn cobblestones where my ancestors had walked. The cobblestones were symbolic for me. They were as close as I could get to my family. I walked where they had walked, where the horses and carts carried their loads. My mother had often described this scene to me and yet I could never quite see it until then.

"Where is Music Street?" I asked Alex after a few minutes of walking away from the main street.

"This is Music Street," he answered as we turned right onto another road.

Why it was only five minutes from the Korzo! I was on Music Street, Gypsy Music Street. The street I had tried to envision for years and years. The street Mother had spoken of over and then over again, and that she had longed to see.

"It was just a short walk to town, a flat walk, our house was at the end of the street," she had said.

The realization hit me. I made it. I actually made it to Music Street. I made my dream happen, and then I broke down into tears. Mark took my arm under my elbow and together we continued walking.

The houses with their front yards full of flowers were all clearly marked. We were looking for number 20. And at the end of the road, there was number 20. But it was not my mother's house. It couldn't be Mother's house because it was new; a beautiful two-story yellow Mediterranean style home that could only have belonged to prosperous people. I was crestfallen. More than anything, I wanted to see Mother's house.

A year before she died, I asked her to draw me a picture of her home. She took a pencil and on the paper I gave her, she drew a small building with four evenly spaced narrow windows.

"Do you remember the number of your house," I asked her.

"Number 20," she immediately replied.

How thankful I was that I had thought to ask for the actual number of her house, something I had never done before even though it seemed I had known the name of the street forever.

But even without the picture, I knew this wasn't the Lehrer home. I was overwhelmingly disappointed, but in that moment I made a promise to myself. I wasn't going to whine about this disappointment nor let it ruin my trip. I told myself it was unrealistic to expect to find everything as it was more than seventy years later. I should be happy to have made it to Munkacs and be standing on Music Street.

Alex knocked on the house next door, number 18; a small drab gray house that resembled the one in Mother's drawing, except it only had three windows. Two women quickly answered the door. One of the women wore a stained checkered dress and was heavyset with short white hair and glasses. She appeared to be in her eighties. The other woman was her stocky middle-aged daughter. She had blond hair swept up and off her face in the heat. She was wearing shorts with a dark tank top and her skin was covered in a sheen of sweat. Both were named Gabriella. They spoke with Alex, and in just a short while we learned their house was indeed Mother's house. Some years back the houses had been renumbered, and the old number 20, Mother's house, was now number 18.

The two Gabriellas talked with Alex as he explained the reason for our visit. They were friendly and welcoming and they did not seem fearful that we would try to reclaim our property. The older woman said she had lived in the house since 1948, only four years after Munkacs was made "Judenrein", free of Jews, in 1944. In 1948, there were many Jews living on Music Street, she recalled. I would learn later that one out of five Jews from Munkacs that survived the war, returned. It was much later, when the Soviets relaxed their immigration policy in the 1970's and 1980's that most of the Jews chose to leave for Israel or the

United States.

The elder Gabriella turned her back to me then. Perhaps it was my imagination, but I sensed that she was trying to hide her face. She was avoiding my eyes, she was remembering war memories. What she saw and heard. Where was she when all the horror was happening? She would have been old enough to remember. Maybe she had found something hidden in the house that belonged to my family. Grandmother stored the Passover dishes in the attic; it's possible they were overlooked in the initial looting of the Jewish homes after the people were forced to leave.

The women invited us to come inside and see the house. They proudly showed us around as Alex translated. He became irritated with me at one point, I was interrupting him.

"I can't translate if you're talking."

"Sorry, sorry," I apologized.

I didn't think. I had never traveled with a guide before, had never needed anyone to translate for me. I was excited and had questions for these women living in Mother's house, a home plundered and then stolen from her family. I wasn't thinking of the logistics of translating; the order of listening, speaking, and then listening and speaking again.

* * *

The women had done some remodeling; indoor plumbing, an additional bedroom. The foyer where we entered had once been the kitchen, the area where my grandmother had cooked for her large family. To the left of the foyer was the original living room, and beyond was an extra small bedroom that closed off with glass French doors. The house was small and dark.

"Only two or three rooms," Mother had said.

"Where did everyone sleep?" I once asked Mother.

"All over," she remembered.

When I put this question to Alex, he dismissed me. "You would understand if you were from this part of the world."

"Where did my grandparents find privacy, a place to be alone together? They had all those children?"

"People find a way to be alone," Alex said. I was sure he was right.

I knew that Mother and her sister Greta, the only two girls, shared a bedroom. It must have been the room with the French doors. The elder woman mentioned that the house used to have four windows instead of the existing three, another detail which convinced me this indeed was the Lehrer home.

The house was messy and when we walked out into the yard we found it terribly neglected. There was the wooden outhouse in the far right corner broken and falling over. Alex said it had probably been rebuilt several times since the war. I imagined my grandfather Markus, swearing to himself as he trekked through deep snow on bitter cold winter days.

To the left of the outhouse was the well. This was where my grandmother drew water to wash and clean. There was another small house in the rear of the yard. This must have been the house the Lehrers rented out, and when there was no tenant, several of the children would "run over there and sleep," Mother had remembered.

It was locked and we were unable to enter and look around. The women said it had been used as a barn, but Alex judged from the construction that it was too nice to have originally been built as a barn. This had to be the rental home Mother had described.

The yard was overgrown and full of weeds. The wood fence was in sad shape as was the wood dog house in the front corner of the yard. An old mangy dog half-hardheartedly barked at us but decided it was too warm to become feisty. Behind what I assumed to be the rental house, was another small new structure built for the elder Gabriella.

"With two women living there, why did the place have to look like that?" Mark later said when we were alone. "My grandmother lived with us and our home was always neat and clean."

The same thought had entered my mind, because this house did not seem typical of the ones we had seen in the neighborhood. Almost all the homes had appeared well kept with nicely tended gardens. I did not want to judge these people. We had stopped by unexpectedly on a Sunday morning. Perhaps the younger woman worked long hours during the week. Maybe the grandmother was in ill health. I did not know their story. I only knew they were kind enough to invite us to see the property, and for this I was grateful.

* * *

We left the house and began to wander the streets of Mukacevo. It was very hot, almost 90 degrees. We stopped to rest and have a cold drink at a cafe, and then we slowly walked down to the Latorica River, only a few blocks from the Hotel Star. The shallow river meandered through the town. On a quiet Sunday afternoon, a few people were swimming, sunbathing, fishing. Two old men played chess under shady trees in the park at the river's edge. There was stillness. Time had stopped for me. To the left was the bridge that connected the town, and to the right, in the not too far away distance were the Carpathian Mountains. A languid summer's day; how often Mother had spoken of this river. In the summer people came here to bathe, to swim, to cool off on days such as this. Some came to the Latorica to wash their clothes.

We traipsed in the heat. The Sunday farmer's market was in progress. Fruits, vegetables and flowers of every color were for sale. People with their shopping bags walked and biked through the streets. Thin, stray dogs ran among the crowd. A woman stopped to pet a small mutt. So, I thought, some Ukrainians do have a soft spot for animals after all.

We walked pass the movie house where Mother used to sneak in to see movies. My grandfather sold wood to this theater, its owner had been one of his customers. Mother walked by there everyday she went to work at the drugstore on the Korzo. Now there were several drugstores on or near the Korzo, old faded buildings with peeling concrete. I didn't know which one was my mother's drugstore, apothecary, as they are called in Europe. Which one, where the druggist made the remarkable skin cream, where Mother wore her important looking white lab coat. Where Chaya Frima Rivka, the only daughter of the famous Hasidic Rabbi Chaim Elazar Shpira, with her plain face and hunched back would stop in to buy cologne for her father. Kolnishe Wasser, created in 1709, this wonderful fresh old world fragrance has been around forever.

The pink building on the corner had once been the mikvah. Perhaps this is where my grandmother would occasionally take Mother for a ritual bath. The large yellow gold synagogue is still there, but only a small part of the top of the building was visible from the street. It was hidden from our view behind a fence, and Alex explained that the Russians had used it for storage. The synagogue was in a state of complete disrepair. The concrete was dilapidated, the roof torn away, paint peeling; a sad, neglected building, a symbol of everything that had happened to the Jews during the war. Once thousands of people had worshiped here, their shul a witness to all the joy people felt on the happy occasions of weddings and bar mitzvahs. Now, nothing left but a shell, a haunted broken shell.

Nearby were the remains of the old cheder, where young Jewish boys studied religion and Hebrew. The building had recently been dismantled along with the entire block, but one of the walls was partially intact. These were the original old red and brown bricks. Perhaps this was the same cheder where some of my uncles had studied as children. I would never know. Munkacs had a large Jewish population, enough to have several cheders. Almost half the population of Munkacs had been Jewish before the war.

We walked along the Yiddishe Gasse, Jewish Street, now renamed Raoul Wallenberg Street. At the corner, on the wall was a small concrete plaque. The Star of David was carved into the tile plaque along with a few lines in Cyrillic. Alex explained this was a memorial honoring Raoul Wallenberg. Someone had attached a plastic wreath of flowers to the plaque, perhaps to dress it up a little; just a small memorial to help remember a very heroic individual. Wallenberg was the courageous young Swedish diplomat who strove to save the lives of so many Hungarian Jews. In a short amount of time, about a year and a half, he issued protective passports and sheltered Jews in safe houses that were designated as Swedish territory. Wallenberg managed to save thousands before his arrest by the Soviets at the end of the war. He disappeared into their prisons and his family never learned his true fate. It was torturous for them, for his mother, and here on the wall was an inconspicuous plaque to mark his memory. But still, I thought, it is something to remind people of his great deeds. And how many people who walk by here everyday actually know or care about the Raoul Wallenberg story, I wondered. And if only there had been more brave people like him, people with a conscience.

***

This street and Munkascy Mihaly Street were the Jewish

ghetto. These were the few streets where the Jews were herded together and forced to live in horribly crowded conditions for a few months before they were deported to Auschwitz.

Across from the Hotel Star was a building with another small plaque on the wall. This was the birthplace of Munkacsy Mihail. His name, date of birth, and date of death were inscribed on the plaque: February 20, 1844 to May 1, 1900. This was the same artist whose paintings we had just seen hanging in the National Gallery of Budapest; moody, atmospheric depictions done in dark shades of black and brown.

* * *

Our first full day in Munkacs and we had already seen so much. It was a wonderful day for me and for Mark as well. But it was also an emotional day, and I was spent. Tired, we waited at least an hour for our dinner. Service can be slow in Ukraine. After a nice piece of trout, a salad and a beer in a lovely outdoor courtyard of a nearby restaurant, we returned to the hotel exhausted. I was tired but could not sleep. I lay in bed recalling everything we had seen, looking forward to the next day, thinking, if only Mother could have been here, to see all this just one more time before she died.

23   Monday, September 8

We awoke to another bright sunny day that promised to be very warm once again. After breakfast, we walked along the Korzo where I bought some wooden souvenirs typical of the type of things made in Transcarpathia: a small carved box and a picture frame with the name Mukacevo carved on it in Cyrillic letters. Both were made from wood. Wood was a big industry in this part of the world and the mountains were covered with trees. Grandfather had cut and gathered his wood in these very hills.

Afterward, we walked over to Mother's house again to take more photographs. I could not stop taking photographs. Alex approached an old man on the street who was walking with a bicycle. He wore a cap above his creased face. Alex asked him if he knew anyone from the Lehrer family. No he did not.

So many brothers, surely there was someone here in Munkacs who remembers at least one of them, I thought.

One of Alex's techniques to find information was to talk to elderly people in the neighborhood where his clients' family had once lived. This man would have been old enough during the war to remember. If he chose to remember; if he admitted to remembering; and if he did not want to remember, I understood.

* * *

We returned to the car and drove to the train station. Mother had started her long journey here. "It took me three days just to get to the boat in Le Havre. First I had to go to Prague to get my visa and from there I went to Paris."

My mother departed forever from her family. She said her good-byes, not realizing she would never see them again.

Somehow, her father knew. "Take a good look at her Roza, because you're never going to see her again," he said.

My grandfather entered the train with his youngest daughter and rode with her for a few stops because it was so hard for him, painful, to say goodbye, Because he had a feeling deep inside himself that this was the last time he would ever see her lovely face.

* * *

We stopped for a few moments to stand in front of the train station, but did not enter the building at that time. When we returned to the car, Mark and Alex were discussing something I had failed to notice outside the station. A woman had lifted up her skirt and relieved herself on a bench. They refused to give me the details but I understood it was a disgusting scene. "Only in Trancarpathia does one see such things," Alex remarked.

Much had changed since Mother had lived in this part of the world. In the old days, gentlemen would bow and kiss the ladies' hands. It was the custom. But surely there had been aberrant behavior, disturbed people wandering the streets. Mother spoke of the nice things, but sometimes she mentioned the beggars, too. Some were "elegant beggars" dressed in old suits. And everyone had a nickname, if someone had a runny nose or a hunched back or any other personal attribute that singled them out from the others.

Alex continued to drive through Mukacevo. We stopped briefly to see the building that once was the Hebrew Gymnasium, the town's Jewish high school. As a small child, Mother never completed the second grade. The truant officer came looking for her at home, saying sternly, "She should be in school."

"I never forgave my mother," she told me once again and for the last time just a month before she died. She grieved this lost opportunity her entire life.

The large Hebrew Gymnasium was painted yellow and green with many windows looking out onto the street where it sat right up close to the sidewalk. I can no longer remember what Alex told us the building is now used for, but I knew it no longer held a crowd of young Jewish students.

We returned to the car and drove to the infamous brickyard. It was on the rail line, the area where the Jews were gathered together and kept under guard for several weeks before they were deported to Auschwitz. There were a series of transports in May of 1944, and within a few days Mukacevo was declared by Eichmann to be Judenrein. For it was the notorious Adolf Eichmann himself who went to Mukacevo; to "get the ball rolling"; to begin the extermination process in the Hungarian provinces before he rounded up the Budapest Jewry. The Russian front was rapidly advancing west and the Nazis were in a hurry to finish their job, to murder as many Jews as possible, before they might be forced to flee.

The conditions in the brickyard were horrendous. The Jews were locked in the warehouse without food and water, without proper sanitation.

We exited the car at the brickyard, a large open space where bricks are still made. The hard red rectangular clay blocks lay scattered in small stacks along the ground under a cloudy sky. At first we saw no one, but then an elderly gray haired man who looked to be a foreman approached us. He was wearing dark gray khaki pants with a blue and white striped shirt pulled taut against a hefty paunch. A cluster of keys hung from his pocket. He spoke with Alex and then Alex translated. The old man knew why we were there, to see the ghetto. I was not the only Jew who had come back years later, to see whatever there was to see, to imagine what had happened in this place.

Alex continued to translate for us as the man spoke. Everything here was the same as it had been years ago, only the warehouse where the people were imprisoned was torn down. As the building was dismantled, the foreman found something he said. It was a gold necklace that someone had hidden between the bricks. Perhaps a young woman hid it because she believed she would return one day to retrieve it. The man must still have this necklace, I thought. Or maybe he had needed money and sold it. What did it look like, I wondered? I imagined a delicate yellow gold chain with a few small dangling pendants. For a brief moment, I had an urge, an impulse, to have this piece of jewelry. The man must give it to me; it could have belonged to my grandmother. I said nothing but the feeling stayed with me. I wanted to have this necklace. I deserved it. This was a tiny connection to everything that was lost and I wanted it. An irrational feeling, or was it? The unsaid words stuck in my throat.

We left the brickyard and drove on and up through the hillside twisting and turning on the roads until we shortly reached the historic Palanok Castle. The castle is a compound of three parts that includes an upper, middle and lower structure situated on a hill above the town. It dates back to the 14th century, perhaps even earlier, and has a long history as a fortress, a prison, a residence for the aristocracy and an agricultural college. Now it was for the tourists to explore.

One tiny room exists within the castle as a Jewish museum. There are a few photographs depicting the atrocities, a few remnants of the Holocaust. There is a list of names of Jews deported from the area, but my family names, Lehrer and Salomon, are not among them.

The castle has beautiful vistas overlooking Mukacevo, the surrounding countryside, the mountains. We take pictures, many pictures, for I may never return to this place although already I feel reluctant to leave.

Back in the town we stopped for lunch at an elegant old world restaurant. Heavy red velvet drapes and lacy sheer curtains covered the windows and dimmed the light in the room. We ate goulash soup with fresh bread. Mother made goulash for our family but she always served it as a beef stew. She added potatoes and the gravy was thicker. Here, as in Budapest, I learned that traditionally goulash is served as a soup rather than a stew. The liquid was not thickened, but still it was delicious.

Alex ate with gusto, his cell phone and tangled keys lay on the table within easy reach. "The two of you, you're very reserved," he said at one point.

"What do you mean, Alex? What do your other clients do? How do they behave?" I asked.

"Oh, sometimes they swear and tell dirty jokes," he answered.

Should I be flattered or insulted? I didn't know any jokes, dirty or otherwise, nor was I in a joke telling mood. This trip was a job for Alex, but for me it was an emotional journey. Later on in the conversation, I forced myself to include an expletive.

After lunch, we drove to the monastery, the same monastery where my grandfather had sold wood. A drizzle quickly turned into a downpour, so we decided to return when the weather improved. Alex took pictures from the car before we left. The monastery was a beautiful old building painted turquoise and green with elaborate white trim nestled in the foothills of the mountains. It sat there, a dreamy image from a fairy tale as we drove away.

We returned to the hotel at four o'clock to rest before dinner. This had been our routine for the past few days. I was having difficulty relaxing. I thought about the town and my mind raced. Mukacevo was charming, prettier than what I had envisioned. Mother had done a good job describing her city," the little Paris of the East." It was larger now of course, a population of 23,000 in the 1940's had grown to almost 85,000 by 2008. Since the end of the war, people from the small surrounding villages moved to Mukacevo, the big city, in hope of finding more opportunities. Old drab homes co-exist with nicer, newer, colorful homes; homes which must belong to prosperous people. And everywhere there are flowers: roses of every kind, every color.

"You know the names of all the flowers," Alex remarked.

I was surprised. I thought everyone knew the difference between roses, daisies and marigolds. The flowers we saw were the same flowers that I grow in my own garden. They were not exotic.

Mother had talked about the fruit trees, and now we saw them full of plums and apples. Nature flourishes here. Lush grape arbors form natural pergolas that provide shade for the patios and entrances of the homes.

Lovely images floated through my mind as I finally fell

asleep.

24   Tuesday, September 9

It was another perfect, clear morning and the day that Alex was going to introduce us to one of the leaders of the Jewish community, a Mr. Abraham Leibovich.

After breakfast, we walked to the new prayer house and community center, just a short distance from the hotel and next door to the large home where Rabbi Shpira once lived. The famous Hasidic Rabbi's grandson, now Rebbe of the Munkacs dynasty located in Brooklyn, stays here whenever he visits during the year.

Mr. Leibovich, a slight, elderly gentleman with graying stubble and a cap to match, proudly showed us around the new buildings. They were modest and clean and painted in shades of bright yellow; well equipped to serve the small, aging Jewish population of Mukacevo.

"There are no weddings, no bar mitzvahs," Mr. Leibovich

explained.

The community is comprised mainly of elderly adults who frequent the center for the meals it provides.

"I'm so happy to find Jewish people still here in this town," I told him through my tears.

We sat and chatted for awhile, but neither he nor the few older people who were eating soup at the tables near us had any information about my family. We promised to return the next day with a donation for the Jewish community.

* * *

We left Mukacevo and drove the four miles to Odavidhaza, the village where my maternal great-grandparents once had a farm. The countryside was pristine; plowed fields, huge sunflower crops and a canopy of leafy trees lined the sides of the narrow road. Alex explained how the farmers live together in the village and then travel to their respective plots of land to plant and tend their fields. In this part of the world, it was common for many Jews to be small scale farmers who owned and worked plots of land. They grew fruit and vegetable crops and raised animals for food.

I did not know how it was when my family had lived here, but I imagined it had not changed much. Mother spoke about her grandmother's chickens and cows, how she loved to visit her in Odavidhaza; how she loved to climb in her bed and cuddle and sleep with her grandmother.

The sun was hot and steady and the village was silent when we arrived. I had heard the family house was at the end of a dirt road near a lake. We never found the lake, but Alex saw hollow ridges in the ground, which indicated that it once held water. Perhaps it had been a river and not an actual lake.

We got out of the car and stood at the end of a road I wanted to believe had been my family's street. Although it was hot, a breeze rippled through the grasses and trees. We stayed in the shade and looked out over the sunny, silent fields with the mountains off in the distance. Ghosts broke the silence and I saw Odavidhaza as it might have been 70 years before. Pious Jewish women with head scarves walked about the village carrying baskets of produce. I saw them working hard in their homes, baking challahs, stirring big pots of food for their large families, bending over washtubs in their yards. Bearded men with their horses and plows could be seen nearby working in the fields....Now there was no one about, but as we drove away a young schoolgirl of nine or ten years, in braids and wearing a backpack, walked by our car. She knows nothing of these things.

We drove up into the mountains and returned to the monastery. Once again it appeared magical and resplendent. In vivid shades of green and turquoise with white ornate trim, it sat tucked into the side of a hill quietly overlooking the city. Later, I learned this building was no longer a monastery, but a womens' convent.

We exited the car and roamed the silent grounds. Another small green church, decorated with paintings of angels and Jesus, was situated nearby next to a tiny cemetery.

Suddenly we were startled. Out of nowhere, a young woman stepped from behind a tree where she had been hiding. Alex translated as this stranger spoke to us in Ukrainian; she needed money for her sick child. She was clean and well groomed and I doubted her story, yet Mark decided to give her something.

Farther down the hill, two nuns were shaking out a small

rug on the sunny lawn. They wore babushkas and long dresses with aprons like the peasant women from long ago. They did not wear the long black habits and formidable head pieces Mother had described, frightening her so much that she would quickly run away.

We drove down the hill and on to the Jewish cemetery. This was the newer cemetery and well maintained. The caretaker greeted us as we entered the grounds. A lean middle-aged man with dark weathered skin, he wore glasses, a soiled cap and shirt. Alex explained we were looking for any family member that might have been buried here; anyone by the name of Lehrer or Salomon. He called out to a woman, his wife, who was standing nearby and explained why we were there. We watched as she hurried off to find the list of names.

* * *

I was not very surprised to discover there was no one from my family here, even though the dated stones revealed many of the people had died before the war. Sarah Salomon, my great-grandmother and a widow, was the only relative I was aware of who had lived in Odavidhaza, at least until she became aged and unable to live alone.

    All the other family Mother spoke about lived in Humenne, a small town now located in Slovakia. It was a few hours train ride away, and sometimes she would visit her Aunt Rose, Uncle Leopold and her many cousins there.

    Most were murdered. Shonye, Itzu, and Emil, a favorite cousin with bright red hair who liked to ride his motorcycle everywhere. There was an Uncle Joseph. He was an American citizen, a traveling salesman who just happened to be back in Humenne when he was trapped in Europe. There were many others whose names I can't recall, but I always remember the story of Piri. There's a photo of my mother as a bridesmaid with Piri on her wedding day and her new husband elegantly dressed in bridal wear. This was the young wife and mother who perished with her four small children.

As for the Lehrers, they died in the conflagration, all in unmarked mass graves. I didn't expect to find them in this cemetery. But yet it was something to see, yes something exciting. A carefully maintained Jewish cemetery, Hebrew letters carved into scores of worn gray slabs, all still standing erect, surviving to show future generations there once was a thriving Jewish community that lived in this part of the world.

We continued to wander about looking at the names and dates on the stones as the caretaker accompanied us. At one point, he casually lifted his finger and pointed to a small unlocked building, a mausoleum. This appeared to be a burial site of someone important.

"Rabbi Shpira, this is Rabbi Chaim Shpira's grave," he said.

Mother had forever reminisced about this famous Hasidic Rabbi. The great, wise scholar who railed against Zionism, who wanted to keep his community close within the confines of Eastern Europe. Here the people would pray and study the Talmud and keep the laws. Their lives would not be diluted or assimilated into the secular world. This was the Rabbi who came to my grandparents' house, pinched my mother's cheek and performed the ritual circumcision on all my uncles. And still today he can be seen in the 1933 video made of his only daughter, Chaya Frima Rivka's wedding. Over twenty thousand guests came from all over Europe and overseas to attend the wedding and the festivities that lasted seven days. In this brief film he lectures to the community about observing Shabbos and the importance of being an observant Jew. Rabbi Shpira died in 1937. He died before life became hell on earth for his people.

We entered the mausoleum and noticed many small paper notes and prayers covering his grave. The Rabbi had had other visitors.

As we were leaving the cemetery grounds, the caretaker suddenly brought out a tall brown glass bottle and poured water over our hands. This was the ancient ritual washing of the hands. Despite everything that had happened in this place, the tradition of washing one's hands after a funeral or cemetery visit still endured. We drove back to the hotel for an early pizza dinner and fell into bed exhausted.

25   Wednesday, September 10

It was our last full day in Munkacs, and we were blessed again with perfect weather. I wasn't ready to leave. Maybe I never wanted to leave. There was a part of me that wanted to stay. I knew it wasn't possible of course, but a piece of me belonged here. These were my roots and they were horribly ripped away. I was frustrated. If I wanted to return with my children it would be an ordeal. Again with the guide, the expense, the remote location of Mukacevo; putting these thoughts out of my head, I decided to enjoy the remainder of the trip and focus on the day ahead.

After our breakfast buffet, we walked to the Jewish community center and gave a donation to the Rabbi as we had promised. Then we drove up into the mountains to see something of the countryside. Within just a few minutes, we were driving though spectacular scenery; rolling lush, vibrant green mountains, little villages off in the distance with their church's spires rising up though the clouds. Hay stacks dotted the fields. The occasional horse and cart joined us on the road. Everything was so pristine, so natural, idyllic. This must have been the way the land looked when Mother walked here. She did not exaggerate the beauty of this place. It was every bit as lovely as she had described.

We stopped at a small roadside building where souvenirs were sold. The Carpathians are a tourist attraction. They had been so in Mother's time and remain so today. In the summer people come to hike and camp and in the winter they ski. Alex suggested anything made from wood was an authentic souvenir. The timber industry was still vital in this area as it had been in my grandfather's time. I chose several carved boxes to bring home to my family. I took many pictures.

On the way back to town, we stopped once again at the railroad station. This time we left the car and went inside to take photographs of the large high ceilinged room. Ticket booths lined the right wall; a big train schedule was posted on the opposite wall. Adjoining the wall was a waiting room with chairs. A few people were sitting and passing the time, waiting for the trains.

Just beyond the large main room, the doors opened to the

tracks. We stepped out onto the platform. This was the very place where Mother had departed, where she had said good-bye to her family, looked at their faces and kissed them for the last time. Her old granny had ridden all night on a train, probably from Humenne since she would have been living with her son by then, to say farewell. And then my grandfather Markus who entered the train with my mother so he could ride a few stops and be with her a little longer before the last good-bye. Had he planned on doing so? Or was it something he decided to do at the very last moment, because it was almost unbearable to part from his daughter.

Back at the hotel, Ala, the secretary from the Jewish community center was waiting for us. A middle-aged woman, her dark lined skin was set off by a mop of unruly white blond hair. She must have been beautiful once, and still with a shapely figure, but something in her face told me her life had been hard. Alex explained that Ala had grown up in a Russian gulag where her father was imprisoned. What had that experience been like? I couldn't imagine.

We had promised Ala a separate donation for her work. She would use the money for programs that involved trying to interest the small population of Jewish youth, in their Jewish roots.

I excitedly explained about the Israeli birthright programs and said

that I would look into organizing a trip for her young people when I

returned to Chicago. Alex translated her response.

"This is not for us," she replied.

I felt confused. Maybe she doesn't understand what I'm

talking about or she's not aware of these opportunities. And what

a wonderful opportunity it would be for these young people, to

have a free trip to Israel. What better way was there to connect

with their Jewish past?

It was months later, back in the States, after many

frustrating attempts on my part to make contact with the right

people, only to come up against silent roadblocks, that I realized

what Ala meant when she said, "not for us." The people who

support the Jewish community in Mukacevo, who helped build the

new prayer and community houses, are the descendants of Rabbi

Chaim Shpira; the same rabbi who opposed Zionism. They desire

to rebuild the Jewish community in Eastern Europe. They do not

want the Jewish people to immigrate to Israel. For in Israel, it is

feared they will become secular, their strict beliefs and traditions diluted in a socialist society.

Later as we took our last stroll on the Korzo, we happened to meet Mr Leibovich. Alex asked him about the drugstores in town and he mentioned that the oldest apothecary was just across the street at the end of the road. We soon found the building and as I stepped inside, I thought, yes, this could be the place where Mother used to work. It was very old with the original dark mahogany counters; mahogany trim along the walls and an old wood clock ticking away the time as it had all those years before. The ladies behind the counter wore white lab coats. I knew Mother wore a white coat at work. The coats made the women look important, and I imagined Mother looking important too, bustling about the shop helping the customers, young and alluring with her dark wavy auburn hair, high Slavic cheekbones and blue almond shaped eyes.

The druggist had sold a variety of colognes and cosmetics and there was one particular skin cream that worked wonders for the complexion. "Skin soft as silk, wrinkles and freckles disappear." In those days, it was one of the druggist's jobs to create the cream. Carefully, he blended the secret ingredients from the formula he closely guarded. But when he learned that my mother was leaving for America, he gave her the formula as a gift.

It was not long after Mother settled in Chicago and started to search among her important documents and papers, that she found the formula missing.

"She lost it," Auntie Greta said derisively.

"She stole it," was Mother's version.

The two "shes," the two sisters, who were always at odds, blamed each other.

Whether the secret formula was lost or stolen will never be known, but the story drifted through our family for years. The rejuvenating skin care formula that could have made millions of dollars for our family. Wasn't Estee Lauder Hungarian? Perhaps Helia D, the cream I had bought In Budapest contained the prized recipe.

People said Mother looked like the actress Ingrid Bergman, some thought she resembled Greta Garbo. I like to think that the druggist was a quiet admirer and that's why he gave her this extraordinary gift.

But of course losing the formula was such a small thing. It really was nothing at all. The horrific devastation in the years that followed Mother's departure; this was the irrevocable loss.

* * *

Outside the shop, in the dazzling sun, we took more pictures. I captured a gypsy boy driving an old wooden horse drawn cart plodding along among the cars in the road.

Then we walked over to Music Street to have one last look at Mother's house.

On the way back to the hotel we stopped to admire the profusion of dense green vines growing everywhere in the alley near the synagogue. Alex took a knife and cut a piece for me. At the hotel, I put the vine in a bottle with some water, wrapped it in plastic and tucked it in my suitcase worrying it would cause problems at the airport. Alex appeared amused that I would have the slightest concern with security. I could sense that in this part of the world the rules were different than what I was used to. I just wanted to bring a little piece of Mukacevo safely home with me. I wanted to try and make this vine flourish so every time I looked at

it, I would recall the wonderful time I had in Mother's town.

26   Back to Budapest

Awake for hours, I had slept very little during the night and had been up since before dawn, too excited to sleep. I laid in bed thinking about the last few days and all that we had seen: Mother's old gray house and it's neglected overgrown yard, the Korzo, the drugstore, the lovely shallow Latorica river that floated lazily through town, the verdant mountains looking down in the near distance. The brickyard ghetto, the train station where Mother said good-bye to her family, the Hebrew Gymnasium, the Jewish cemetery, Odavidhaza, Palanok Castle, the monastery; I had to leave it all. I got up from bed and looked out the window. The Catholic church's spire towered above the rooftops of the city. I did not want to leave. I wasn't ready to leave.

Mark wasn't having any of it. "Bye by my love, bye by," he joked as he packed his bag.

He wasn't planning on staying, and of course neither could I.

* * *

Alex drove us back to Budapest after breakfast. He drove as he had done on the way east, at the breakneck, harrowing speed of 100 miles an hour. And while he drove we listened to his tapes. The Beatle's *Yellow Submarine* was playing. Alex's thick head and neck bobbed back and forth keeping time with the music. One chubby hand tapped out the rhythm on the steering wheel while he ate sunflower seeds from a plastic bag by his side with the other. We sat silently listening to the music, Mark in the front seat and I in the back. I was tired, my hair wet from the shower, I was cold from the air conditioning Alex had cranked up in the car. I sat with my jacket over my head. I wished only to think about everything we had seen and done and savor it all.

Just as we made it safely through the border into Hungary, Alex got a speeding ticket. This will surely temper his driving I thought, but I was wrong. Once the police were out of sight, Alex continued to drive as zealously as ever.

Relieved to be back at the hotel, we thanked Alex.

"Why didn't I think to ask my mother more questions, does

everybody say this?"

"Yes, everyone says this," Alex replied as we said our good-byes.

He had been a competent and knowledgeable guide and we were grateful for all his help, but we needed some time alone, some down time at that point. We were leaving soon, our flight scheduled for the following day. I wanted to relax a little, to digest everything.

We had gained an hour upon returning to Hungary. It was still early afternoon in Budapest and the weather was warm as we walked the Vaci Utca and then settled down at an outdoor cafe. We ordered a few beers and unwound from the past two weeks. We were going home the next day. Our dog Sandy, our family pet of fourteen years would not be waiting for us.

This trip had been a dream come true for me. Sadness, joy and excitement mingled together. How I wished Mother could have joined us on this trip and seen Munkacs one more time. I don't believe she would have been sad about seeing her old town. I think she would have been as excited as I was, to welcome the ghosts that lingered on the streets and haunted the homes; the

spirits that swam in the river and walked in the mountains.

27   Home Again

One of the first things I did within a week of returning home was drive by my old neighborhood. I was looking for Jerry. It was late September, still warm and sunny but with a hint of autumn in the air. There he was in his driveway. There was a ladder and tools and the garage door was open. He was doing chores outside around the house, the most mundane chores any helpful husband would do. It all looked so normal. I parked the car and quickly walked up the driveway as I called out to him before I lost my nerve.

"I've just returned from Mukacevo Jerry, I finally made the trip."

"Ah, Mukacevo" he said, as he walked towards me smiling, surprised at my unexpected visit.

"Can I ask you something Jerry?" And then I asked the question before he had time to respond. "Were you there when

they took the Jews away? Did you see what happened?" This a
question that I had never dared to ask of anyone, especially from
the only uncle of the three who had survived the war, and who
was sane enough to tell me something before he died.

And Jerry simply nodded his head, "Yes I was."

"Please tell me."

* * *

"I was fourteen years old and I was the Shabbos goy of
Turka. I lit the candles and stoves for the Jews on their Sabbath.
One day the Nazis entered and surrounded the town. It was just
like what you read about but even worse. No one could escape.
The Jews were rounded up. They were numb. They prayed. I had
a crush on Chana, a Jewish classmate. She shared her lunch with
me. They took her with her family and shot them all. I never got
over it."

Jerry's eyes began to water as he became emotional.

"Did you ever see any acts of kindness?"

Jerry looked up at the sky as he remembered. "There was

an SS officer who fell in love with a beautiful Jewish girl. One morning they were both found hanging."

They had killed themselves rather than face the horror their future most certainly held. How is suicide an act of kindness, I wondered.

Jerry continued with his story. He had become separated from his family and two of his sisters were murdered, one by the Nazis and the other by the Communists. He ran and hid and despondent, he contemplated suicide as well. During the latter part of the war he was able to connect with the Allies. Because he was fluent in German and Russian, they employed him in their intelligence unit. This was why he never attempted to visit Turka when it was still part of the Soviet Union. At the war's end Jerry immigrated to the United States. It would be four long years before he found his brother and both parents whom he had believed were dead.

Jerry had recently returned from a visit to Turka. A mass grave where his sister had been shot and buried was uncovered. Jerry had placed a memorial with her name, Olya, in the town's church.

"The Jews were numb," Jerry said again. "They didn't resist. Why didn't they fight? If it had been me I would have done something."

Still the same old irksome argument, I felt too drained to try and explain "why" to him. There were so many reasons why many of the people went along without resisting, but for me as for my mother the foremost answer is this. Even in their nightmares they simply did not, could not conceive of the hell that lay ahead; the unimaginable, inhumane, malevolent cruelty.

"Who would believe that such a thing could happen in the twentieth century," Mother brooded over and over again through all my years growing up. "And no one did anything, no one helped them. The whole world looked on and did nothing."

This was the answer to Jerry's question that I could not bring myself to say.

The Jews were taken with force at gunpoint. They were beaten, intimidated, humiliated and starved. To ensure their compliance, their hopes were raised by false promises of being sent to work camps. They had no weapons to defend themselves, nor did they believe people, often their neighbors with whom they had lived for years, held such intense antipathy toward them or were capable of perpetrating such horrific crimes. The European Jews understood their situation was dire, but the extent of the direness was unfathomable. They had suffered through bad times before, were inured to them. Things would improve if they were patient.

Now they were trapped and lied to at every turn until it was too late to do anything but die.

Jerry said, "I don't mow my lawn on Shabbos out of respect for them. The Jewish people here in Highland Park, they drive their BMW's, their German cars."

What was Jerry's meaning? Although the people have been schooled in the history of the Holocaust, perhaps it doesn't resonate for them. They're out of touch with the endless evil that occurred, and could well occur once again under the right circumstances. I resented Jerry's condescension. I left his yard deciding I would not return for that cup of coffee he offered "should I drop in anytime."

Our family had a funeral cortege for Sandy. Mark carried her ashes in a small white tin box decorated with gray paw prints in which the vet had returned her to us. He and I, Matt, Hedy and Jolie walked up to the bluff overlooking Lake Michigan. This was her favorite place to run and play catch. There we said good-bye to our beloved pet as we placed her ashes inside the ring of the magical tree of seven trunks.

28 Remembering

More than two years have passed since my trip to Mukacevo. It's a cold winter and snow is falling outside my window. I think of Mother's town nestled in the foothills of the Carpathian Mountains. It's winter there as well. The town must be blanketed in heavy snow, the rooftops covered in white. It's just a few days before Christmas. I imagine people shopping on the Korzo looking for gifts for a cherished family member, nothing too expensive for I see the people in old worn coats bundled up against the cold. They don't have much money to spend, it's poor in this part of the world. A lovely carved wood box like the ones I bought would make an excellent present for someone.

And when I close my eyes, I see Gypsy Music Street. Thick drifts of snow lay on the ancient cobblestone streets, and there is Mother, walking away from number 20. The snow is falling faster, the wind is starting to pick up but Mother keeps walking, hurriedly walking in the snow as she loved to do. And she never looks back.

29 Auntie Greta Dies

It was a hard thing, difficult to let go of the last surviving old aunt who had been a part of my life for so long. Feisty and flirtatious almost to the end, Auntie Greta died at 103 years old, in the spring less than a year after Mother. There had been no reason to tell her that Renee had died the previous summer. By then she was confused most of the time, her mind addled by age, so why bother to upset her with this news during the little time she was lucid.

When my sister Junie or I would visit with her in those final months, and in those moments when she could think more clearly, she would ask about Mother.

"I want to call her but I can't hear anything anymore and she can't hear me either. How is Renee?"

We lied. We made excuses. It was easy to do now because Auntie Greta herself was fading. But Junie thought she knew.

"I can tell from the way she looks at me. She knows."

* * *

Once, I asked Auntie Greta about her family, her parents in Munkacs and what she remembered of them.

"That vas a terrible story, to take people and kill 'em. I vas so vorried," the smile left her face, the light in her eyes was gone.

That's all she said, and then we quickly spoke of other things.

Greta had left behind a boyfriend in Munkacs, Elemer. She said she had loved Elemer, just not enough to stay in Europe and marry him. She loved more, the fact that she was leaving on a ship for America. After her death, looking through old papers, her son Eddie found a letter from Elemer written in Hungarian. Eddie had the letter translated and gave me a copy.

Elemer wrote Greta the winter before her departure. She had gone to Humenne for a few weeks, to say good-bye to the aunts, uncles and cousins before she left Europe for America. In the photo, Greta is seated on the far left.

Elemer's letter was filled with longing and love:

"I can't even express in words how I miss you, my dear beloved. When the train rolled out with you from the station, I was standing there for a few minutes as a living corpse........How much I will cry when you leave, that's better not to think about, I start shivering even if I just think about it..........I don't know if you leave for America whether I go crazy."

And with his entreaties to her to write more frequently, because perhaps she was already distancing herself from him:

"My dear Gizike, if you love me, you will write me more often, if possible everyday.......write to me more. Loving you and

thinking of you forever, your Elemer."

"Vell, I didn't sleep vit him," Auntie Greta said when I asked about their relationship 65 years later.

On my aunt's 101st birthday, Mark and I stopped at her home unexpectedly with a gift. Greta was flustered; she wasn't dressed for company she said, although she seemed happy enough to see us. Her daughter, my cousin Cookie was there for her daily visit, and we all sat down together to chat and drink tea. I became engrossed in conversation with Cookie and hadn't noticed that Greta was absent from the room.

"Where did your mother go?" I asked.

"Oh she's probably putting on her makeup," and within a few minutes my aunt emerged from the bathroom wearing lipstick, rosy cheeks, a hint of blue eye shadow and mascara. She looked pretty; she always wanted to look pretty. At 101 years of age she still cares how she looks, it's important. There is a lesson for me, I thought.

30   Israel 2011

We traveled to Israel for the first time to see Ruth and Elisheva, the twins, my cousins, tough sabras, they were orphaned at fourteen years of age and left to raise themselves. It was they, the daughters of Chaim, the only brother who had immigrated to Israel, who had for years encouraged us to visit. There had never been a good time. When we lived in Geneva, we started to plan a trip, but in 1986 the intifada exploded and with three young children, I quickly lost interest. The trip was put on hold.

And as the years passed, the Middle East was always in a state of political tension or turmoil. The history of the region was convoluted and confusing, I really didn't understand much. The idea of this trip was overwhelming, yet it was Mark who had wanted to travel to Israel instead of going to Eastern Europe.

"Why do you want to go to those places after what they did to your family?" he asked.

But it was only because I did make that journey, and see the ghetto streets, and stand in the brickyard, and look out to where I knew the train tracks were, that I truly had a desire to go. This was the land of the diaspora and it was destroyed, the people annihilated. I needed to see something else, something better for the Jewish people.

* * *

In the few months preceding our trip to Israel, I read what I could about the region, but the copious material was difficult to absorb. The historical, the biblical, I wanted to have at least a rudimentary understanding of the things I would see. And despite my mother's religious background, my Jewish education had been sparsely meted out. I silently fretted.

31   Shalom

But something very special and unexpected happened when we finally did arrive in Tel Aviv, and Elisheva opened her door. "Shalom" she greeted us, and I saw my mother's face. The face of a Lehrer, for Elisheva bore an uncanny resemblance to my mother in her younger, prettier years; red hair, small almond shaped blue eyes, freckles and fair skin. The mannerisms were there as well; her body language as she read the newspaper or prepared delicious dinners.

"It's like your mother is making supper for us again," Mark said.

I could see my family's face here in Israel, and it was wonderful.

* * *

Elisheva, Leo, Ruth, and Moti took turns showing us the sights in and around Tel Aviv for a few days, before Mark and I would take the bus to Jerusalem.

I remembered Moti's story, how he was thrown into the streets of Budapest at six years of age. His sister who was taken in by a Christian family, and sent to church, had a difficult time readjusting to living life as a Jew.

"We had a lot of trouble with her in the beginning," Moti said.

Moti appeared calm, quiet, and unflappable. He is a retired engineer now, but he participated in many of Israel's wars serving in the IDF, the Israeli Defense Forces, and I know he had experienced much hardship; saw death up close, knew real fear that many people never know in their lifetime.

"If there had been an Israel, those horrible things would never have happened," Moti remarked.

So my cousins are busy with their grandchildren now, helping their families as much as possible, for life in Israel is hard.

"None of us here, our friends, none of us had grandparents, so we are running and doing as much as we can.

We can't do enough for our grandchildren," were Elisheva's words.

They're still young enough and strong enough to fill their families' lives with support and love. There will not be a needless void.

From left, the author, Ruth, Shiry (Eli's daughter) and Elisheva

* * *

We're in Yad Vashem, the Holocaust museum and memorial. In the entrance, on a large screen hung up on the wall, is the 1933 video of Munkacs. Children are singing, young Zionist men and women are dancing the hora. And after touring the exhibits inside the museum, we walked outside and down into the Valley of The Communities; red and beige cavernous rocks carved with the names of five thousand communities where the significant Jewish populations were destroyed.

"Where is Mukacevo?" I asked a stooped elderly woman who was wearing a name tag and wandering nearby. She appeared to be museum staff.

"A little to the left," she pointed with a crooked finger.

And not far, around a bend in the narrow lane, we saw a rock with the large letters: MUKACEVO.

It was a joy to see my families faces in Israel, for they were the same faces that had seen so much persecution and oppression in other lands; places where Jews were murdered senselessly. Mother frequently ruminated about her father's remark, an observation.

"We are just guests on this earth," he used to say. But tragically, my family like millions of others was forced to leave this life way too soon.

Anger, irredeemable loss, resentment; those feelings never go away.

"We have a small family," Mother often apologized to guests at our dinner table, "Seven brothers, all vanished." People were missing from the dinner table.

In Israel the Jews are tough, they're strong, and they carry guns to defend themselves. They know how to make the desert bloom. They can hold up their heads and be proud. And when they say "never again," they mean it.

* * *

Never a day goes by that I do not think of my mother and her lovely little town, Mukacevo, "the little Paris of the East." I always think of how it must have looked as she was growing up, and how it looked when I visited more than 70 years after her departure. It is said that Europe stays mostly the same. The physical landscape doesn't change much; it's the people who disappear.

I will be forever grateful that I was able to experience part of Mother's world; a fragment that is only fabled in the imagination of most. Family stories are handed down through the generations. These towns and villages are the settings of books and movies.

People often read the stories and see the movies but for whatever reason, most do not travel to these places. I am fortunate that I could afford the trip and that I had the chutzpa to make the trip, for it was one of the highlights of my life. I am also fortunate to have such a wonderful husband who was willing and excited to share this amazing adventure with me.

About The Author

Roberta Dietzen is currently working on a collection of short stories. She lives in Highland Park, Illinois with her husband Mark.